Messages of
God's Abundance

Also by Corrie ten Boom

Reflections of God's Glory

MEDITATIONS BY THE AUTHOR OF *THE HIDING PLACE*

Messages of God's Abundance

FOREWORD BY CHARLES SWINDOLL

Corrie ten Boom

Zondervan

Grand Rapids, Michigan 49530 USA

Zondervan

Messages of God's Abundance
Copyright © 2002 by Stichting Trans World Radio voor Nederland en België

Requests for information should be addressed to:

Zondervan, *Grand Rapids, Michigan 49530*

Library of Congress Cataloging-in-Publication Data

Ten Boom, Corrie.
 Messages of God's abundance : more meditations by the author of The hiding
place / Corrie ten Boom.
  p. cm.
 Sequel to: Reflections of God's glory..
 ISBN 0–310–24570–2 (hardcover)
 1. Christian life–Reformed authors. I. Title.
BV4501.3.T454 2002
242 — dc21   2002006574
                                                                          CIP

This edition printed on acid-free paper.

Interior design by Laura Blost

Printed in the United States of America

02 03 04 05 06 /❖ DC/ 10 9 8 7 6 5 4 3

Contents

Foreword

by Charles R. Swindoll

Every time I think of it, I'm humbled to the core. I'm both wounded and healed. Injured and restored. I'll tell you the truth, nothing levels me quite like . . . forgiveness.

It happened a short time ago in Israel. I was leading an Insight for Living tour through the painful halls of the *Yad Vashem*, the Holocaust Museum of Remembrance. Each horrifying photograph and caption illustrated in detail the depths of man's sinfulness and also the suffering of individuals and a nation. Dachau. Ravensbrück. Auschwitz. They are no longer words to us—they are wounds.

Stepping outside the dank, gray dimness of the museum and into the warm sunlight provided welcome refreshment. There, lining the path outside the building was the Avenue of the Righteous Gentiles, a lush, tree-lined walkway celebrating individuals who helped rescue Jews from Nazi atrocities. Each tree had a simple plaque at its base, stating the name and country of the honored Gentile. Beside many of the trees were piles of stones, stones of remembrance, put there by people the world over who simply wanted to say "thank-you."

In that bright sunlight, each lost in our own thoughts, we walked the rows of trees. I looked for a friend's name—a woman who has been like a mentor to me in her message of grace and forgiveness. And when I found it, overcome with emotion, I placed a small stone atop the pile. The plaque read: Corrie ten Boom, Holland.

Those of you who know her story as told in her book, *The Hiding Place*, know the message she lived was learned in the schoolroom of suffering. This is always true of forgiveness. It is impossible to experience forgiveness without having endured a measure of pain—the pain of either being offended, or the pain of knowing you have offended someone else. For Corrie, this word of offense was Ravensbrück.

Few had more right to feel bitter than Corrie, yet few have reflected God's forgiveness any greater than she did. How did she do it? How could she forgive those who killed her family, who robbed her of everything?

I thought of this question the following day in Jerusalem. As I stood near the spot where our Savior died, I remembered His words from the cross: "Father, forgive them. . . ."

In the shadow of the cross—with its vertical beam to the sky and its horizontal beam outstretched—I was reminded of forgiveness: both vertical (God's forgiveness of me), and horizontal (my forgiveness of others).

And I knew how Corrie could forgive. She saw it modeled.

I had the privilege of pastoring the church where Corrie attended during her final years. I remember her saying on one occasion that, as children of God, we must be like a mirror, holding up a reflection of God for the world to see. The light doesn't come from us, it's a reflection of His glory. When they see us love, they see a mirror of God in our lives. I'm convinced, especially after standing in that bright sunlight outside the *Yad Vashem*, that nothing reflects God's love and grace greater than when we forgive.

As you know, Corrie's story had only begun when the war ended. Upon her release from Ravensbrück until her death in

1983, she traveled the world encouraging the church and proclaiming the Gospel to the lost. Thanks to the ministry of Trans World Radio, she also became a pioneer of Christian broadcasting. In a wonderful twist of events, her message of grace and forgiveness beamed across Europe and even into Germany via the radio transmitters built—but never used—by her enemies to spread Nazi propaganda! I've visited that infamous building in Monte Carlo that we often have called "the Hitler building" and couldn't help but smile at God's wonderful and inscrutable ways. Who could have guessed in those vicious days of war when that tower was erected that it would be used to broadcast a message of healing and forgiveness to the post-war world?

The same is true today. In the United States, as well as around the world through Insight for Living's partnership with Trans World Radio, we receive countless letters and messages from people who tell us how *Insight for Living* has been a mirror of God, reflecting His provision for their individual needs. We marvel at God at work. I join with my friends at Trans World Radio in continuing to pray that, through *Insight for Living* and other broadcasts teaching God's Word, this very personal medium of radio will give you hope and encouragement, and help you through the very personal issues of faith and forgiveness.

I was so pleased when my friends at Trans World Radio told me about these newly found meditations from our friend Corrie that have never been in print! The first of these "lost writings" were compiled in the book, *Reflections of God's Glory*, and now continue in this book you hold in your hands, *Messages of God's Abundance*. These are both worthy titles considering the life and message of this dear saint of God. I smile when I read these pages, hearing in my memory her rolling Dutch accent and seeing her wise and clear blue eyes, "Pastor *Svendahl*, do all to the glory of God."

May you, too, hear her message in these pages and in so doing, give all the glory to God.

Charles R. Swindoll
Chairman of the Board, Insight for Living
July 2002

Acknowledgments

Special thanks to:

Rinse Postuma, director, Trans World Radio voor Nederland en Belgie (Netherlands and Belgium), for special permission to translate and publish the manuscripts in English;

Clara M. van Dijk, retired, Trans World Radio voor Nederland en Belgie, for championing the initial vision for this book and organizing, researching, and editing the original Dutch manuscripts;

Claire L. Rothrock, Trans World Radio—Europe, the Netherlands, for translating all materials from Dutch to English and turning it into a labor of love;

Hans van der Steen, retired director, Trans World Radio voor Nederland en Belgie, for his valuable assistance to this project and for sharing many insights into the life and ministry of Corrie ten Boom gained from his personal relationship with Corrie formed through years of coproducing her radio broadcasts;

Tom Watkins, Trans World Radio—The Americas, for initiating and overseeing this project, and for editing the final manuscript.

Introduction

No matter what the denominational label on our church door might be, by our hearts we are all known by the same name: "The Die-hard Independents!" God says to us, "Your ways are not my ways," and of course we agree—and carry on our own way. "My thoughts are not your thoughts," and our mouths voice their approval—but we never doubt that we know best. Sooner or later, though, if we are truly to build something that lasts for God's kingdom, God must write His words not just on the surface of our lives but down in the depths. It is exactly people like Corrie ten Boom that He uses to do the writing.

Humanly speaking Corrie was weak. No money, few connections, no public relations machine, no fame. All she had was her weakness, a word that doesn't fit easily into our normal vocabulary. It's the opposite of what we call success. Surely to be weak is to fail. It's like ... well, like a man nailed onto a cross to die. How could *that* possibly achieve anything? All Corrie had was her weakness. Oh, and one other thing: her Lord—crucified, risen, in heaven, and by her side. She simply believed, really believed, that with Him everything was possible, and she passed her days putting that belief into practice. Her weakness became a door through which Jesus stepped to do His all-powerful and perfect will.

Many will know the story of Corrie's life (told in the book and film *The Hiding Place*, and in other books she wrote), how she helped Jews to escape the Nazi regime of World War II, was betrayed by two fellow Dutchmen, and sent eventually, after two imprisonments in Holland, to Ravensbrück concentration camp in Germany. Her experiences were terrible but uniquely equipped her for the post-war role as God's ambassador of love and forgiveness around the world, which became her consuming passion. Men could do their worst, but with a certainty that none could deny or ignore she knew that in the end "Jesus is Victor," the phrase that became her watchword for life.

Corrie's first contact with Trans World Radio was in 1965, and within a year Dutch-speaking listeners in the Netherlands were hearing her radio talks broadcast from the powerful transmitters in Monte Carlo, which TWR has used since 1960. Ironically, it was the Nazis who built these transmitters but never used them; clearly God had other plans! Later her voice was heard by listeners in the Dutch Antilles and in Africa.

But English listeners and readers would never have had access to this storehouse of spiritual treasure had it not been for the tireless efforts of Clara M. van Dijk, now retired from Trans World Radio—Netherlands, who organized these materials and championed the vision for seeing them published, first in Dutch, and now in English. In 1997, TWR staff member Claire Rothrock began her translation of all of Corrie's manuscripts. Twenty-four talks were gathered together and published by Zondervan in 1999 as *Reflections of God's Glory*, and now this second and concluding volume adds a further twenty-six fine meditations to the series. A new generation is discovering to its delight and blessing the warm biblical wisdom that was Corrie's trademark.

Trans World Radio began broadcasting Gospel radio in 1954 and today sends out more than 1,800 hours of programs every week in 180 languages and dialects around the world. By utilizing thirteen super-power transmitters, stretching from the heart of Europe to the Pacific Ocean, as well as by using satellites, the Internet, and more than 1,600 local radio stations and transmitters, TWR is the most far-reaching Gospel broadcaster in the world today. A million and a half responses are received each year from listeners in 160 countries. We praise God for this growth and that many who might never have heard of God's love for them can today hear the Gospel and be strengthened in their faith through radio. And we thank Him too for giving us people like Corrie ten Boom through whom His love speaks so clearly and so powerfully.

Listeners loved Corrie's radio talks, and they were easily the ones that prompted the most letters from Dutch listeners. I suspect this was because people loved *her*. The Spirit of Jesus hung about her in a way that made His love radiate through in almost a tangible way. She has fairly been called one of her generation's most loved women.

From my desk I can see a photograph of the Birkenau concentration camp in Poland, the near neighbor of the more famous Auschwitz. The electrified fence and the watchtowers are still there as necessary reminders of the horror that they once looked down on. But now there is also something else. The parade ground that once held broken, shivering bodies is now carpeted with beautiful wildflowers. Overhanging the fence are the verdant branches of many willow trees, dancing and singing in the breeze. God is steadily taking back that which men had arrogantly tried to claim as theirs alone. It is a picture of life bursting forth out of death, and it is a picture of Corrie ten Boom's life and the lives of those she touched.

There are some Bible verses in which the apostle Paul wrote about Abraham, but they seem to me so applicable to Corrie (forgive me for changing "he" to "she"):

> Yet [she] did not waver through unbelief regarding the promise of God, but was strengthened in [her] faith and gave glory to God, being fully persuaded that God had power to do what he had promised.

Corrie exemplified those words throughout her life. Reading the pages of this book you'll be in the company of a woman of faith whose life gave, and still gives, glory to God. My prayer is that through them God will write deeply in all of us and will change our allegiance once and for all from "The Die-hard Independents" to become those who, like Corrie, give glory to God!

David Tucker, President, Trans World Radio
Cary, North Carolina
August 2002

꒦

One

Let Your Light Shine

꒜

In Matthew 5:13 and 14–16 we read that the Lord Jesus says, "You are the salt of the earth," and "You are the light of the world. A city on a hill cannot be hidden. Neither do people light a lamp and put it under a bowl. Instead they put it on its stand, and it gives light to everyone in the house. In the same way, let your light shine before men, that they may see your good deeds and praise your Father in heaven."

I have spoken to prisoners in many countries. During the war I experienced what it means to sit behind a door that can only be opened from the outside. Maybe that is why I am so interested in prisoners and sympathize with them so much. I think of a rough young man in Mexico, who had an eighteen-year sentence. You don't get that for just stealing a car. But something had happened in his life. The Lord Jesus had laid His hand upon him. He prayed, "Come into my heart, Lord Jesus" and Jesus came. That's what it says in Revelation 3:20, "Here I am! I stand at the door and knock. If anyone hears my voice and opens the door, I will come in." And that had happened. The man became an evangelist in his prison. When I arrived there, he had already brought half of his fellow prisoners to the Lord.

I hope that you, the reader, will get to heaven and that I will meet you there. Then I am sure that I'll be able to introduce you to quite a few fervent evangelists whom I met in prisons, fellows who were serving their sentences. But not only that, we will also find many who, through them, found their way to heaven.

I want to tell you something I learned from a prisoner in New Zealand. Sometimes you hear the most wonderful sermons from people who are serving their sentence in prisons. I had preached on the text, "You are the light of the world." Can you say that to prisoners? Wouldn't it be better to say, "You are the darkness of the world"?

One of the men who had heard my sermon said, "This morning I was leafing through the Bible and I found the story of three murderers. One was called Moses, one David, and one Paul." Were they murderers? Yes. We know them as God's heroes, but all three were murderers. The prisoner said: "Mates, there's hope for you and me." What can God do with a murderer who surrenders totally to Him? What can God do with a completely surrendered "decent" sinner like you and me? Will you surrender to Him? Miracles will happen. You will become the light of the world and the salt of the earth.

Let's pray together. "Lord, I thank You that You can use sinners. You didn't call the angels to be evangelists; they have other work to do. But You can use me. Lord, hear those who listen and are saying: 'Can You use me?' Take my life, and let it be consecrated, Lord, to Thee. Oh, Lord, how wonderful it is that You will make them the light of the world and salt of the earth. Hallelujah. Amen."

Two

Two Kinds of Love

B ecause God has poured out his love into our hearts by the
Holy Spirit, whom he has given us" (Rom. 5:5). An ocean
of love and light covered an ocean of sin and darkness when
Jesus said on the cross, "It is finished."

There are two kinds of love: human love and God's love.
Human love can fall short; God's love never does. In 1 Corinthians 13 we read about divine love. In the original Bible text
there are two different words for love. Human love is called
philia, God's love is called *agape*. God's love is the greatest reality, here and now—not only if we live in a beautiful house and
have enough to eat, but even if the very worst happens in the
life of a child of God, the best remains, namely God's love.

I experienced that love when I was imprisoned in a concentration camp during the war. Each morning they held roll call.
The supervisor used that time to demonstrate her cruelty. One
morning I could hardly bear to see and hear what was happening in front of me. Then a lark started to sing in the air. All the

prisoners looked up. I looked up too and listened to the bird, but I looked further and saw heaven. I thought of Psalm 103:11, "For as high as the heavens are above the earth, so great is his love for those who fear him." I suddenly saw that the ocean of God's great love is greater than human cruelty. God sent the lark every day for three weeks to teach us to direct our eyes to Him.

When I was released and went back home, my body carried the scars of the camp for a long time. My friends were afraid that I would say: "The greatest reality in life is human cruelty." But through God's grace I was able to say: "There are three great realities in life. The first is the ocean of God's love in Jesus Christ; second, God's promises; and third, God's commandments."

There is nothing in which God demonstrates His love more clearly than in His promises and His commandments. The amount of God's love is unlimited, but we only receive as much as we use. A tradesman once complained that he was so busy he could hardly bear it. He was a child of God and I said to him, "How wonderful that you don't have to do it alone." "What do you mean?" "Well, what a friend we have in Jesus." "Do you really think that I have time to think of that?"—He looked like a mountain climber who has a guide with him and says to him, "Don't you see how hard it is to climb this mountain? Do you really think I have time for a guide?"

I, too, often get so busy with my work that I have no time to think of Jesus' love. I become impatient and unkind. How much I still have to learn! I cannot gain the victory over life's problems, big or small, by my own strength. When I was in the concentration camp, I sometimes felt hatred rising inside me, but the Holy Spirit taught me a prayer: "Thank You, Lord Jesus, that You have brought God's love into my heart through the Holy Spirit whom You gave me. Thank You, Father, that Your love in me is stronger than all hatred." And I found that there was no longer any room in my heart for hatred.

God wants to conquer our largest and smallest difficulties through His love. Think of the problems in your life at this moment. Are there problems that you cannot conquer with human love? Do it from now on with God's love, God's "agape," which never falls short. "Happy is the man who can draw his love from the heart of his Savior," Count Zinzendorf once said.

A pastor once spoke of God's conquering love in Jesus Christ. A mentally handicapped boy, Toontje, who went to church faithfully but could never understand the sermons, listened this time with great happiness. The pastor forgot the rest of the congregation and spoke only to Toontje, whose face began to beam more and more. He understood something of the ocean of God's love. The next morning the pastor planned to visit Toontje, but he heard that the boy had died in his sleep. There was an expression of heavenly joy on the face of the dead boy. The pastor said: "I believe that Toontje's heart was broken because he tried to grasp too much of God's love." God, who is so great, loves to give great gifts; but oh, we people have such small hearts. But the Holy Spirit continually makes our hearts greater and stronger, until we one day see Jesus face-to-face.

When we are on the beach we only see a small part of the ocean. However, we know that there is much more beyond the horizon. We only see a small part of God's great love, a few jewels of His great riches, but we know that there is much more beyond the horizon. The best is yet to come, when we see Jesus face-to-face.

"Thank You, Lord Jesus, that You poured out God's love in our hearts through the Holy Spirit. Thank You, Father, that Your love conquers today's problems. Hallelujah. Amen."

Three

Working,
Inspired by God's Love

I have often spoken about witnessing. We can all be used by the Lord to bring others to Him. That can be quite difficult, and sometimes even very dangerous. In countries where there is no freedom, we may have to die for the Lord. That is not so strange. Even now there are many martyrs who are imprisoned or killed for their witness.

But it is so wonderful that the Lord Himself gives us courage. I remember a story that I heard about a missionary who was going to China. It was still possible then, but it was dangerous. Someone asked her, "Aren't you frightened?" She replied, "No, there's only one fear in my heart. In the Bible it says that a grain of wheat must die to bring forth fruit; now I'm only scared that I'll become like a grain of wheat that isn't prepared to die."

I have to tell you about a boy who worked with me in the underground movement during World War II. His name was Piet Hartog. He was a very brave assistant of mine. I remember that one day we heard that Jewish children in an orphanage in Amsterdam were to be murdered. I called together the boys I worked with and said, "You have to save the children." And they did. My boys got the children out of the orphanage; and my girls distributed them among many families—all in one day. It wasn't very difficult. Just imagine holding a baby in your arms and saying to someone, "Do you want to save this baby? If you don't do it and I can't find anyone else, this baby will be killed." Of course the person will say, "No, no, no, give me the baby."

Piet Hartog said to me that evening, "I believe that we are involved in the most important work there is, saving lives from morning to evening. I don't want to go back to college. This is really essential work. It is wonderful." I said to Piet, "I too am so happy when I think of those babies; but, Piet, do you know that there's even more important work, not only saving lives but souls—showing people the way to Jesus." Then Piet laughed, and said what someone who hears this may say or think: "I am a Christian boy; yes, I'm a Christian. I read my Bible, I pray. I go to church. But telling other people about the Lord Jesus, that's the pastor's job." I said, "Piet, every child of God is called to present the Gospel, and in your life a time will come when you will see that's the most important thing for you!"

Six months later Piet ended up in jail and heard he had only a week to live. The day before he was shot he wrote us a long letter: "All the boys and men in my dormitory are condemned to death just like me. I am so happy that I was able to tell them that if they accept the Lord Jesus as their Savior, He will make them children of God; that a child of God may trust that, if he believes in the Lord Jesus, in the house of the Lord with its many mansions there is one for him. I think it's so wonderful that I could tell them that they only need to tell the Lord of their sins and they will receive forgiveness. The blood of Jesus will cleanse them of their sins. Now I know that presenting the Gospel is the most important thing for every child of God."

I have a message from Piet Hartog for you. Are you a Christian? Don't wait then like Piet Hartog did, to the last week of your life, but say to the Lord today, "Take my life, and let it be consecrated, Lord, to Thee." If you do that, the Lord will use you to tell others about the Gospel. The marvelous thing is not just that we may do it, but that we don't have to do it in our own strength. We only need to tell the Lord and He will do it. We only need to look to the Lord and He makes us, as it were, a mirror of His love. He has such longing and such love for the lost. If we let Him speak through us, then that love enters our hearts. Oh, how wonderful that is. If you do it, and you see people around you later in heaven, some of them will say, "You invited me." If you hear that, you will know that you didn't live in vain.

Let's pray together. "Thank You, Lord, that You want to use us, 'decent' or 'offensive' sinners. If we come to You, You will make us the light of the world. Hallelujah. Amen."

Four

What Do You Reflect?

And we, who with unveiled faces all reflect the Lord's glory, are being transformed into his likeness with ever-increasing glory, which comes from the Lord, who is the Spirit.

—2 CORINTHIANS 3:18

I once had an accident in my hometown. The police helped me and took me away by car. Whenever a policeman in Holland does anything, a report has to be submitted. So out came his notebook and he asked my name. "Corrie ten Boom." He looked up in surprise and asked, "Are you a member of the Ten Boom family we arrested during the war?" "Yes, I am." During that time many good policemen were forced to work for the German Gestapo; they stayed in their positions to help political prisoners. The man said, "I'll never forget that night. I was on duty when the whole Ten Boom family and about forty friends were arrested because they had helped Jews. There was an atmosphere of celebration in our police station rather than a gathering of prisoners likely to die in prison and concentration camps. I often still tell of how your father took out his Bible and read Psalm 91 and then prayed so calmly."

Ten years later the policeman still remembered which psalm my father had read: "He who dwells in the shelter of the Most High will rest in the shadow of the Almighty. I will say of the LORD, 'He is my refuge and my fortress, my God, in whom I trust'" (Ps. 91:1–2).

I like to fantasize about heaven; I know that reality will be a trillion times more beautiful than our wildest dreams. But one thing I know from God's Word, the Bible: we will recognize each other there. Did Jesus say to His disciples on the Mount of Transfiguration, "May I introduce Moses and Elijah?" No, that's not what happened, but the disciples still knew who Moses and Elijah were. Why? Because they had glorified heavenly bodies and in heaven we will know each other far better than we did on earth.

When I see my father again in heaven, I'll ask him: "Do you remember the night we were all together in the Haarlem police station?" He is sure to say, "Yes, I remember that; that was the last night we were together on earth." Then I'll ask him, "Do you remember the policeman who was on duty?" Most likely he will say, "No, I don't recall him." That night Father didn't think, *Now I have to say or do something that will be a blessing to that policeman.* Father was always very relaxed, even in the prison where he died after ten days. Father's whole life was focused on Jesus, and Jesus made him a mirror of His love and His glory.

A mirror doesn't have much to do. To do its job it just must hang or stand in the right direction. You and I don't have to do a great deal either. We need only to look to the Lord Jesus and He will make us like mirrors, and He does it so well! We don't need to strive and try to be a blessing but just look in the right direction. Then Jesus makes us a mirror of Himself. When you get to heaven, people may say to you, "You invited me here." Then you will ask, "When did I tell you about heaven?" You will discover that Jesus used you when you were really looking to Him.

We are moons, not suns. The moon only reflects the light of the sun. We need only to reflect light; then we live to His glory.

I looked to Jesus and the dove of peace flew into my heart. Then I looked at the dove of peace and it flew away. In which direction are you looking? To your faith? In Hebrews 12:2 we read, "Let us fix our eyes on Jesus, the author and perfecter of our faith." Our faith is not the power but the instrument by which we can use the power of God. I have a small dictating machine. If it's not working properly, I don't repair it myself. I send it back to the manufacturer. If my faith isn't working, I send it back to Jesus, the maker and perfecter of my faith. When He repairs my faith, it works.

Which way are you looking? To your sins? Oh, turn your eyes away from your sin and look to Jesus; then you will find grace. Jesus died for your sins on the cross. He died for you. He lives for you now. If you have sinned, bring it to Him and His blood will cleanse you of all sin and unrighteousness that you confess (see 1 John 1:7–9). In which direction are you looking? To your concerns? The Bible says, "Do not be anxious about anything, but in everything, by prayer and petition, with thanksgiving, present your requests to God. And the peace of God, which transcends all understanding, will guard your hearts and your minds in Christ Jesus" (Phil. 4:6–7).

Peter could walk on the waves as long as he looked to Jesus. But as soon as he looked at the waves, he sank. If you look to Jesus, the waves in life's storms become like firm ground. Yes, you and I must look in the right direction: away from our sins, away from our worries, and even away from our faith in Jesus, only to Jesus Himself. Who directs our gaze in the right direction? The Lord Jesus Himself does. Through His Holy Spirit He directs our gaze and makes us mirrors of His peace and His light.

"Hallelujah, what a Savior You are. In You we find solid ground, in which we can sink our anchor forever. Amen."

Five

Who Is Lord of Your Life?

Dear Father, in Jesus' name we pray that You will make things a little clearer about what it means to be ready for the great day that is coming when Jesus Christ, Your dear Son, will come on the clouds of heaven. Thank You for telling us so much about that in Your Word. Help us to understand it better through Your Holy Spirit. Amen.

꙳

What does everyday life have to do with the second coming of Jesus? Everything, because the Lord could come back today. We don't know the day or hour, but we also don't know a day or hour in which He cannot return. The Lord Himself said that we have to watch for the signs of the times. If we look at world history through the window of the Bible, we know that many signs are apparent in the newspapers. But the wonderful thing is that from God's Word we know that He is interested in us in microscopically tiny things and also in great things. No hair of our head will be lost and God has the universe in His hand. Therefore we need not fear, even if the earth gives way and mountains fall into the heart of the sea. Let us be prepared when the time comes. In what condition will the Lord find us? In what condition will the Lord find you, find me, if He should return today?

I was once visiting a farmer in Australia. He told me that in a nearby village there was a woman of faith who would be wonderful for me to meet. The farmer told me of the many times she had given him advice and how much she knew of the Bible. We had an hour to spare, so we went to visit her. I was expecting a lot in that village, so far away from the city and the rest of the world. I was eager to find this woman who lived close to the Lord.

The hour I spent with her was a disappointment. She talked only of what modern theologians had said, written, and done. She was outraged. She recited all their errors in great detail. At the end of the hour I said, "Well, we haven't had any time to pray together, or to tell something of our own walk with the Lord." We can be led by a spirit of criticism, just focusing on others' wrongs—however unorthodox they may be.

Our hearts can be so ready for battle with those who think differently that it makes us gloomy. Yes, I know we must distinguish between spirits. We are in the days that "false Christs and false prophets will appear and perform great signs and miracles to deceive even the elect—if that were possible" (Matt. 24:24). I am so happy that it says "if that were possible." It is not possible!

We need the Spirit's fruit, yes, and indeed, its gift of discernment of spirits. But that is different from a spirit of criticism, which is always hard-hearted. Led by a spirit of criticism, we set ourselves up to judge fellow Christians who don't think the same way about the inspiration of the Bible, the gifts of the Spirit, or the Millennium. It doesn't help them and it doesn't help us.

Do you have a criticizing spirit? How do handle your money? Are you trying to avoid paying taxes? The ways you use your money are important. How is your marriage? Is it pure? Do you demonstrate love, understanding, tolerance, and forgiveness toward others? You say you can't do it? God can. His love never fails. Romans 5:5 says God's love has been poured into our hearts through His Holy Spirit. Here is the answer again: If there are difficulties, be filled with God's Spirit.

A woman complained of great difficulties in her marriage. Life with her husband was hard, and she was sometimes infected with his darkness. I taught her to pray in her heart, "Thank You, Lord, for Romans 5:5. Thank You, Lord Jesus, that You have brought God's love into my heart through the Holy Spirit. Thank You, Father, that Your love in me conquers my husband's darkness." I met her sometime later, and she said, "My husband has changed completely." Yes, of course he had changed! She had demonstrated God's love to him.

We cannot do it. But He can. We conquer through the blood of the Lamb. You must ask the Lord today, "Is there anything in my life, in my heart, of which I would be ashamed if You returned today?" If the Lord says there is something, repent, because the kingdom of God is at hand.

"No one can serve two masters," the Lord Jesus said at the very beginning of His time on earth. I spoke on this text in a very primitive church in Africa. I felt I wasn't getting my message across. I started walking. The church had a very uneven floor. With my left foot on the high side and my right foot on the low, I walked crookedly down the aisle. It was hard going. When I got back to the pulpit I said: "Did you see how awkwardly I was walking through the church? That's it: serving two masters! It's not easy, and it's very dangerous too." After the sermon, a school principal came to me and said, "I now see that I am walking like a cripple in my marriage, in my personal finances, and with my colleagues at work." He repented of his sin.

Are you walking crippled through life? Keep that up and you will be ashamed when Jesus returns. Give yourself to the Lord and ask Him to fill your entire heart. I once asked an old lady if she wanted Jesus to fill her heart. But she started to tell me that she was very old and very sinful. She could talk of nothing else. I realized then that I had to make things very clear to her. I told how the Lord Jesus says in Revelation 3:20: "Here I am! I stand at the door and knock. If anyone hears my voice and opens the door, I will come in and eat with him, and he with me." I said to the old woman, "Imagine a time when I utterly lack the energy to keep my house clean. I just can't take care of it. Then you come to visit me. When you come in, you see can how dirty everything is. But you also see that I don't have the strength to houseclean, so you say, 'Give me a dust rag and a broom.' And you clean it all up."

The old lady's face began to beam with pleasure when I described such a wonderful role to her. "And then after you have cleaned the house you say, 'I will make a cup of tea and visit with you.' You see, that is what the Lord does. When He comes into our hearts, He sees that they are dirty. He doesn't say, 'I will come back some other time when the house is clean.' No, He cleans it Himself. He purifies us with His blood, and then it is clean. He comes to live in us, He wants to be one with us, and He is host and visitor at the same time." The elderly lady suddenly understood, and with happiness she asked the Lord to come in. The wonderful thing is, Jesus loves us so much, He does it. And He who began a good work in us will carry it on to completion until the day of Christ Jesus.

"Thank You, Lord Jesus, that when You tell us to be pure, You purify us Yourself through Your Spirit. Show us, Lord, if there is anything in our hearts of which we will be ashamed when You return. I praise and thank You, that if we confess our sins, You are faithful and just and will forgive us our sins and that Your blood cleanses us of all sins. Hallelujah, what a Savior.

"Yes, Lord, come quickly, and do what You have promised. Make all things new, so that the earth will be full of the knowledge of the Lord as the waters cover the sea. Prepare me for that great and glorious day when You return. Amen."

Six

When It's Hard to Forgive

λ

Some time ago I was with a condemned man in his cell. He was a black man who had been arrested just the day before and was to die the next day. He was, indeed, executed the following day. It was during a political uprising in Africa, and many people were killed. He had been treated roughly. I could see red welts and wounds. There was nothing in the cell other than a plank on which we sat side by side. I could see his handcuffed hands. We had a good conversation, however, because he, too, was a Christian. He had the hope of heaven. He had brought his sins to the Lord Jesus, and we could talk wonderfully about Jesus who loves sinners and who gives us eternal life.

But then I asked a question: "Can you forgive the men who brought you here?" "No," he said, "because they are the reason I am to die." "Yes, I can understand that very well; but I have to read to you what the Lord Jesus said in the Sermon on the Mount: 'For if you forgive men when they sin against you, your heavenly Father will also forgive you. But if you do not forgive men their sins, your Father will not forgive your sins' [Matt. 6:14–15]. The Lord Jesus said that." "Yes, but I can't do it," the condemned man said.

I then told him about an experience I had during World War II in Holland—how a man, whose wife I tried to free from jail, betrayed me. Because of his betrayal, my whole family was jailed and several of them died there. I had hated that man. When I realized I hated the man, I was shocked. The Bible says, in the Sermon on the Mount, that hatred is actually murder. "You have heard that it was said to the people long ago, 'Do not murder, and anyone who murders will be subject to judgment.' But I tell you that anyone who is angry with his brother will be subject to judgment" (Matt. 5:21–22). In verses 44 and 45 it says, "But I tell you: Love your enemies and pray for those who persecute you, that you may be sons of your Father in heaven. He causes his sun to rise on the evil and the good, and sends rain on the righteous and the unrighteous."

When I understood that I hated the man, I brought my hatred to the Lord. Here is the marvelous thing: if we, as children of God, know that we have sinned, then we also know the path to take. We know what we have to do. In 1 John 1:8–9 it says that if we confess our sins, the Lord is faithful and just and He will forgive us our sins and will cleanse us from all unrighteousness that we have confessed. So I did that very quickly. Then the Lord cleansed my heart with His blood, as it says there too. If a heart is cleansed by the blood of Jesus, then He always wants to fill it with His Holy Spirit—and the fruit of the Spirit is love.

In Romans 5:5 it says that the love of God has been poured into our hearts by the Holy Spirit. That love is also love for our enemies, as a fruit of the Holy Spirit. After the war, the Lord used me to bring that man to conversion. He had been sentenced to death because he had caused the death of many people by betraying them. I was able to write to him and tell him that I had forgiven him. That was because of God's love dwelling in my heart. The man then said "Yes" to Jesus before he was executed.

When I told all this to the man now sentenced to death, he saw the light and said, "Oh, but it's true—I can't do it, but Jesus can!" We went to Jesus together, and that man forgave his murderers—because actually they were his murderers. He had not done anything wrong himself, but he had become caught up in politics. I later heard that he sent his wife a message that same day. He wrote, "Forgive the people who brought me here. You can't do it, but Jesus can; and we have to do it because the Lord Jesus taught us to." I was so happy that he had understood. The following day he was killed; but he had been able to write to his wife.

Now I have to ask you something: Can you forgive? Can you forgive the one who stole your husband's or your wife's love? Can you forgive the rival, who through dishonest competition, ran you out of business? Can you forgive the people who slandered your good name? You can't do it; I can't either. But Jesus can. If you forgive your enemies, you will touch the ocean of God's love as never before.

Isn't it wonderful that Jesus is the victor? I have found it more difficult to forgive a friend who has acted as an enemy, than to forgive an outright enemy. Not so long ago, I had forgiven someone, but the feelings kept coming back. I brought it to the Lord again, but it came back yet again. I felt discouraged. Then I learned this excellent image from a friend. We have all heard church bells ring. But in the moment after they have stopped, you can still hear "ding-dong" and again "ding-dong." Those "ding-dongs" are like the echoes of anger. The echoes may continue even when you mean to stop, but if you bring the "ding-dongs" confidently to the Lord then they will truly be silenced. Jesus is the conqueror. Shall we thank the Lord for that?

"Oh, Lord Jesus, how wonderful it is that You don't just tell us to love our enemies, but, through Your Holy Spirit, You give us the love that You ask of us. Show us, Lord, if there is a corner of our heart with a little bitterness—or maybe a lot of bitterness. We thank You, Lord, that if we bring it to You knowing that it is a sin, You forgive and cleanse us. Thank You that You fill a cleansed heart with Your Holy Spirit, and that the fruit of the Spirit is love—love even for our enemies and for friends who have behaved as enemies. Thank You, Lord, that You make us more than conquerors. Hallelujah. Amen."

Seven

Be an "Up-to-date" Soldier

꒯

Every child of God has a task in this world. As this world is becoming darker and darker and more disordered, it is good for us to be aware of the task we have received from our Master. He said, "You will be my witnesses in Jerusalem, and in all Judea and Samaria, and to the ends of the earth" (Acts 1:8), and: "You are the salt of the earth . . . the light of the world" (Matt. 5:13–14).

When the Lord gave us such a big plan of action—to the ends of the earth—He first told us how we would be capable of being witnesses: "You will receive power when the Holy Spirit comes on you" (Acts 1:8). Without the Holy Spirit we can't be light, salt, or witnesses. Not in the street where we live nor in the place we work, neither close to home nor far away on the mission field. But we can be powerful through the Holy Spirit, wherever we might be called. The world needs powerful children of light! We have to be up-to-date. The antichrist is marching firmly on with his great army. If the children of light stand idly by, we will be in great danger.

I believe that the kingdom of God is obstructed more by indifferent Christians than by the vigorous marching of the antichrist. A Vietnamese boy once said to me, "Sometimes churches are mousetraps for Christians. They meet there, enjoy the Word and fellowship with the Lord and each other; but they forget that they have been called to spread the Gospel message over the whole world." He is right. There are churches like that. But I am reminded of Oswald Smith's church, a church that is alive, where the people are fed richly, and where they have warm fellowship with each other. I think they have sent out more than three hundred missionaries whom they fully support. No, Oswald Smith's church isn't a mousetrap.

Do you want to join Christ's army? In 2 Timothy 2:3 we read, "Endure hardship with us like a good soldier of Christ Jesus." Do you want to become a soldier in that army? There is an army that is so powerful, so well-armed, and under such perfect leadership that victory is assured. That isn't an army that is fighting for a particular country. It is a world army. Do you know what the future of the world is? A kingdom of peace, of peace on earth equal to that in heaven. An earth filled with the knowledge of the Lord as the waters cover the sea, where swords will be beaten into plowshares. More details can be found in the words of the prophets, the words of the Lord Jesus Himself, and of the apostles, and also in the Revelation of John.

I once heard a story about Napoleon. A new group of soldiers had signed up and he addressed them like this: "Men, if you fight in my army, you can be sure that often when you are hungry there will be no food. In bad weather, you won't always have a roof over your head. You can expect blood and sweat, but I can assure you of one thing; if you fight for me, then you dedicate your life to Napoleon who has never lost a battle.

Think for a minute. If you want to be a soldier in my army, take a step forward." He turned his back to them and waited for a minute. Then he turned back round and looked at the young men. They still stood there shoulder to shoulder. He said, "I'll give you one more chance. Isn't there anyone who dares? I will wait one more minute." "You don't need to," one of them cried, "we all took a step forward." But Napoleon lost his final battle.

King Jesus will never lose. He was a conqueror, He is a conqueror, and He will be a conqueror. He Himself warned us, "I tell you the truth, unless a kernel of wheat falls to the ground and dies, it remains only a single seed. But if it dies, it produces many seeds. The man who loves his life will lose it, while the man who hates his life in this world will keep it for eternal life" (John 12:24–25). Yes, it can mean martyrdom. Peter says in 1 Peter 4:12–14, "Dear friends, do not be surprised at the painful trial you are suffering, as though something strange were happening to you. But rejoice that you participate in the sufferings of Christ, so that you may be overjoyed when his glory is revealed. If you are insulted because of the name of Christ, you are blessed, for the Spirit of glory and of God rests on you."

I was approached by a young man in a country where it was very dangerous to follow Jesus. We had listened with the whole church to what the Holy Spirit had to tell us about following Him who had come from heaven to this earth and had lived here, and then died on the cross at Golgotha because He loved us so much and wanted to save us for eternity.

. The young man said, "Now I am prepared to live and die for Jesus if that is what He wants." I read in the young man's eyes the Spirit of glory of which Peter had spoken. The purpose of the global battle in which we find ourselves is "Peace on Earth." John wrote in Revelation 21:3–5, "Now the dwelling of God is with men, and he will live with them. They will be his people, and God himself will be with them and be their God. He will wipe every tear from their eyes. There will be no more death or mourning or crying or pain, for the old order of things has passed away." He who was seated on the throne said, "I am making everything new!"

The marvelous thing about the commission of our Lord Jesus Christ is that not one of His followers needs to be excluded. Every person is either a missionary or a mission field. The Lord Jesus died on the cross for the whole world, and whoever believes in Him will not be lost. But He said more: "Anyone who has faith in me will do what I have been doing. He will do even greater things than these, because I am going to the Father" (John 14:12).

How can that be? You and I doing greater things than Jesus did? Yes. Do you know why? He went to the Father and He is there at the right hand of the Father on the throne of God. He does greater things than He did in the three years that He worked on earth in Palestine, and He wants to do it through you and me. No one is excluded. Maybe you are sick or elderly, or perhaps you can't even go out anymore; but the commission of the Master is for you too! In the service of King Jesus there is no unemployment.

I have seen many old peoples' homes in the world; some were sad, some happy. The happiest and most joyful home I have seen was in the Mike Martin community of Seattle. There were large grounds with various buildings. In one was a boys' school, in another a conference center; and in one of the many other buildings was an old peoples' home. Over one hundred elderly people lived together there. If something happened in the community—for example, Johnny fell down the stairs in the boys' house—the first call was to the doctor, but the second phone call was to the old peoples' home. As soon as the old folks got the message: "Johnny has broken his leg," they started to pray. They prayed for Johnny's healing, for wisdom for the doctor treating him, and for the nurse who would take care of Johnny. The old people participated actively in this way. When they heard I was to visit them for a week, they prayed every day for three weeks for a blessing on the event, and it was exceptionally blessed. There were several missionaries sent by that community and they could count on the continuous prayer of the old people in the home!

Intercessory prayer is never lost. In the book of Revelation, chapter 5 verse 8, it says, "And when he had taken it, the four living creatures and the twenty-four elders fell down before the Lamb. Each one had a harp and they were holding golden bowls full of incense, which are the prayers of the saints." Now you know, just as well as I do, that the atmosphere in an old peoples' home can sometimes be very dejected. There is disappointment and loneliness. But in that old peoples' home in Seattle I saw the happiest elderly people I have ever met. Praying as an intercessor is a blessing to yourself, and that is actually the case with all the work you do in obedience to the Lord Jesus. If you pass on the light to others, then it shines in your own heart too.

Let's pray. "Lord Jesus, forgive us if we have seen and thought so little of the Great Commission—the task of being witnesses throughout the whole world, to the very ends of the earth. Thank You that You forgive us if we bring this negligence to You. You have said that if we confess our sins, You are faithful and just and will cleanse us of all our sins through Your blood. Yes, Lord, cleanse me too of these sins. I thank You that from now on You allow me to work in Your kingdom—each in his small corner and I in mine, wherever You may call us. Thank You. Amen."

Eight

Missionary or Mission Field

꒰

Everyone is either a missionary or a mission field. If you have never opened your heart to the Lord Jesus, you are a mission field. I say to you: Reconcile yourself to God. Come to Jesus; bring all your sins to Him. He died for you on the cross and says, "Come to me, all you who are weary and burdened, and I will give you rest" (Matt. 11:28). Jesus will give you rest and answers to your problems now; redemption, deliverance, and eternal life—because you become a child of God. Now a child of God is called to be a light of the world; so listen to what I am going to say to missionaries, because you, too, become a missionary if you say "Yes" to Jesus.

A missionary has in mind the welfare of all he can reach, and in 1 Corinthians 12:7–10 it says, "Now to each one the manifestation of the Spirit is given for the common good. To one there is given through the Spirit the message of wisdom, to another the message of knowledge by means of the same Spirit, to another faith by the same Spirit, to another gifts of healing by that one Spirit, to another miraculous powers, to another prophecy, to another distinguishing between spirits, to another speaking in different kinds of tongues, and to still another the interpretation of tongues." What riches!

Are these meant for you and for me? Yes, of course. Paul says to each one of us in 1 Corinthians 14 that we should eagerly desire the gifts of the Spirit. Yes, that's what a missionary has to do! How important it is for us to reach out for those gifts, as God describes them through Paul in 1 Corinthians 12 and 14. Then we will really experience in practice the rich promises that Jesus gave shortly before He ascended to heaven: "You will receive power when the Holy Spirit comes on you" (Acts 1:8). That power, among other things, consists of the gifts of the Holy Spirit.

But we need to remember that between 1 Corinthians 12 and 14 is also chapter 13. There Paul writes that even if you have all the gifts but not love, you have nothing! In addition to the gifts of the Spirit there is also the fruit of the Spirit. Galatians 5:22 says, "The fruit of the Spirit is love, joy, peace, patience, kindness, goodness, faithfulness, gentleness and self-control." Remember, all these promises are in Jesus: Yes and Amen (see 2 Cor. 1:20). The gifts and the fruit of the Spirit are for you and me. Everything is actually summed up in Romans 5:5, "God has poured out his love into our hearts by the Holy Spirit, whom he has given us."

Some time ago I was in Israel. There was a lot of hatred and fear in people's hearts. One evening a boy came up to me after a service. I had spoken about the ocean of God's love, with which we come into contact through the Lord Jesus and how that love is available to us every day if we give the Holy Spirit room in our hearts. The boy said, "I thank God for today's message. The Lord has taken away all the hatred from my heart.

I can now forgive others completely. I tried before, but I couldn't do it; now I can do it through the Holy Spirit."

I remember speaking to a man in Germany. There was a darkness about him. He approached me after a meeting. Suddenly I recognized him. He was one of the guards in the Ravensbrück camp where my sister died and I suffered terribly. When I saw him, I remembered all the cruelties he had committed. At first, I felt bitterness in my heart. But then something happened. The man told me, "At Christmas I found the Lord Jesus. I brought all my sins to Him and I sought the grace to ask one of my victims for forgiveness. That's why I came. Will you forgive me for all those cruelties?" It was as if a stream of forgiving love surged through me. I was able to shake that man's hand. It was love through the Holy Spirit—because if you forgive your enemies you experience the ocean of God's love as never before.

Let's pray. "Thank You, Father, in the name of Jesus for the tremendous riches that are ready for us, if we just accept them by faith. Thank You that all the promises in the Bible are for us. Thank You that we can fulfill our mission call—not in our own strength, but in Your strength. Give us many opportunities. Will You open closed doors? Will You take all doubt and confidence in ourselves from our hearts, and instead of that give us faith and trust in You, through Your Holy Spirit? Amen."

Nine

A Message of Abundance

Then Jesus went up on a mountainside and sat down with his disciples. The Jewish Passover Feast was near. When Jesus looked up and saw a great crowd coming toward him, he said to Philip, "Where shall we buy bread for these people to eat?" He asked this only to test him, for he already had in mind what he was going to do. Philip answered him, "Eight months' wages would not buy enough bread for each one to have a bite!" Another of his disciples, Andrew, Simon Peter's brother, spoke up, "Here is a boy with five small barley loaves and two small fish, but how far will they go among so many?" Jesus said, "Have the people sit down." There was plenty of grass in that place, and the men sat down, about five thousand of them. Jesus then took the loaves, gave thanks, and distributed to those who were seated as much as they wanted. He did the same with the fish. When they all had had enough to eat, he said to his disciples, "Gather the pieces that are left over. Let nothing be wasted." So they gathered them and filled twelve baskets with the pieces of the five barley loaves left over by those who had eaten. After the people saw the miraculous sign that Jesus did, they began to say: "Surely this is the Prophet who is to come into the world."

—JOHN 6:3–14

I was able to speak twice in an East African prison. People listened very carefully. I felt as those disciples must have felt when they fed those five thousand people—from just five loaves and two fishes. The secret was, they had accepted that meager meal from the hand of the Lord Jesus. A full basket of leftovers remained for each of them. What foolishness, yes, a foolishness of God. In 1 Corinthians 1 and 2 it says that the foolishness of God is wiser than human wisdom. The foolishness of God is the greatest wisdom.

Imagine the disciples attempting this feat with human wisdom. They might have said, "There is far too little for all these people; let's eat it ourselves. We need to keep up our strength, and we don't want to be undernourished." I imagine that those few loaves and fish would have left twelve healthy young men very hungry still. But now, through the foolishness of God, there was a basketful for each disciple! A good meal, after the effort it took to distribute food to five thousand hungry people. Abundance for all. How marvelous.

I experienced the disciples' joy when I saw those men in Africa, with their broken lives, sitting on the ground in front of me. I told them about the ocean of God's love and that there was One who died on the cross out of love for sinners to carry our sin and guilt. I told them what Jesus said: "And surely I am with you always, to the very end of the age" (Matt. 28:20). Our Savior did not only die, but He rose again and lives for us today. I told them: "Among a million others, He also sees each of you. There is One who loves you, who loves you so much that He wants to fill your heart with His Holy Spirit, and the fruit of that Spirit is love, joy, and peace. He says: 'Here I am! I stand at the door and knock. If anyone hears my voice and opens the door, I will come in and eat with him, and he with me' (Rev. 3:20)." Many of the prisoners answered the knock; they opened their hearts to Jesus. He came in, because that is what He said He would do. There was joy among the angels of God (see Luke 15:10).

At the end I asked, "Do you have any questions?" Two prisoners stood up. One asked, "Don't you have a medicine against sin?" I said: "Yes, the blood of Jesus Christ washes away all sins that you confess; and then, when your heart has been cleansed, He will protect you with His blood. In the book of Revelation it says that they overcame by the blood of the Lamb. You can't understand that—neither can I—but it works, and I know that from experience." Then I said to the other prisoner, "What did you want to ask?" He said: "Yesterday you came here, we were hungry and you gave us a lot of food. Today you came again; we were even hungrier, and you gave us even more. But what about tomorrow?"

I discussed the prisoner's question with some African Christians. I asked, "Will you bring these hungry people spiritual food? Many were born again in the past two days, but they are very weak babies in Christ and they need food and care." An African answered, "But we can't do that; we have no car. We must walk; that will take up most of our day." The Lord Jesus said: "I was sick and in prison and you did not look after me"(Matt. 25:43).

That night one of the Africans had a dream. He had a new-born baby in his hands. He looked at it with admiration and love. Then he saw that the baby was about to die, and he was saddened. When he woke he asked, "Lord, what does this dream mean?" The answer was: "That was one of the babies who was born again in prison; it died from lack of food and care." The African called his fellow Christians together and told them his dream. They decided that one of them would visit the prison each Sunday.

May I ask you a question: How far is it from your home to the closest prison? Do I mean that you have to go and work for the prisoners? No. I don't intend it as a criticism. I needed to live behind the walls of three different prisons before I could feel I wasn't too sensitive for such dismal work. So I can understand if you don't dare to do it. But I hope you will read Matthew 25 again; the Lord might want to speak to you through it. This chapter isn't just about prisoners but also about those who are hungry, strangers, and the sick. It can be an eye-opener.

I once received a letter from a German man under a life sentence. He wrote, "Once a month I am allowed to write a letter, but I don't have anyone to write to in the whole world. Could I write to you?" What loneliness. I was deeply moved. Of course I could have replied "Yes." But I am a wanderer, sometimes I travel in countries where post only reaches me very slowly, if at all. I also understood that this man was one of the many lonely people who live behind closed prison doors. I brought the letter before the Lord and He gave me wisdom.

I asked on the radio if there were any people who might write occasionally to prisoners who receive little or no mail. People responded, but they were the prisoners—they so eagerly wanted mail! Oh, that work progressed so wonderfully after the war! If you too want to get involved, write to a prison and ask for an address. It is such a wonderful opportunity to share the love of the Lord Jesus for sinners and show them the way to start a new life. Intercession is very important too, and prayers for wisdom.

Let's pray together now. "Father, in Jesus' name we pray for all the prisoners who are behind closed doors, which can only be opened from the outside. But, Lord, You said in the Bible that You have imprisoned the prison (see Ephesians 4:8 KJV). I know from experience, Lord, that in prison we can be free if we are but united with You. Will You speak to all the prisoners who listen to Christian programs, and say to them: I am here, I live, and I want to be your Friend, your Redeemer. Lord, I know that You will not send away anyone who comes to You.

"Lord, listen too to those who are free but who have suddenly realized that there is work to be done in Your kingdom, and who say: 'Take my life, and let it be consecrated, Lord, to Thee.' If You think it is right and that they need to write to a prisoner, will You tell them? Thank You, Lord, that later on You will say to these people: 'I was in prison and you visited Me.' How wonderful that will be! Make us faithful and resourceful through Your love. Thank You, Lord Jesus. Hallelujah. Amen."

Ten

Are You Living on Petty Cash or a High Bank Balance?

I once broke my arm in a car accident. It was very painful. It troubled me that I couldn't bear it. I screamed and cried because it hurt. I was ashamed. I had just finished my book *Marching Orders for the End Battle*. I had written that a child of God has to be strong—and can be strong because the Lord wants to give us what we need. But now I lay there in utter misery and I was weak.

A visitor came and said, "Stop trying to be strong. You just need to stay close to the Lord. He will take care of it." That was liberating. I had tried, but when I stayed close to the Lord and was aware of His presence—the presence of Him who said, "Surely I am with you always, to the very end of the age" (Matt. 28:20)—then I was able to bear the pain.

Sometimes we try to manage on our own resources. Imagine you have a large business and therefore a large bank balance, and a big bill arrives. It would be stupid for you to pick up your wallet to see how much money you had, or if you went to other people and said: "Please check how much money you have with you. How much can we raise together to pay this bill?" No, you would simply write a check and the bill would be paid. It is so wonderful that we may live on the bank balance of the Bible—a bank account that is never frozen.

Every person is either a missionary or a mission field—the people in your office, school, or hospital, and your neighbors. Perhaps you say I have really tried to be a missionary to them, but I couldn't because their doors were closed. I can well imagine that you weren't able to open them, because you can't do that if you are living on your own petty cash. But with the Bible's bank account, we depend upon the foolishness of God, which is much wiser than human wisdom; then we can see that Jesus can enter through closed doors (see John 20:19, 26).

The people around you are in need. They don't know that Jesus died on the cross for the sins of the whole world, including their own sins—and that if they bring their sins to Him, He will wash them away with His blood. We must learn not to depend on the wisdom of the wise, but on the foolishness of God. Then the impossible happens, like the five thousand people in John 6 who had to be fed by the disciples with only a few loaves and fishes. They took it from the hand of Jesus and passed it around—and then, after distributing the food, there were twelve baskets of leftovers!

The Bible's bank balance is extremely high. I am going to mention a few checks: "Who is it that overcomes the world? Only he who believes that Jesus is the Son of God" (1 John 5:5). Another check says: "I will instruct you and teach you in the way you should go; I will counsel you and watch over you" (Ps. 32:8).

Or where Jesus says: "I have come that they may have life, and have it to the full" (John 10:10). The Lord Jesus didn't say, "You will receive power if you do your very best, and then go forth and teach all nations," but He said, "You will receive power when the Holy Spirit comes on you" (Acts 1:8). Then He gave the Great Commission: "You will be my witnesses in Jerusalem, and in all Judea and Samaria, and to the ends of the earth" (Acts 1:8). The Holy Spirit dwelling in us can do it. It says in the Bible: be filled with the Holy Spirit (see Ephesians 5:18).

I have a glove here. It can't do anything, but if I put my hand in it, it can do a lot: writing, sewing, and much more. Now I know of course that it isn't the glove, it's my hand in the glove. You and I are like gloves, and the Holy Spirit is like the hand— it can do a great deal. If I ball my fist in the middle, the glove flops limply. Each finger has to be filled. Therefore, the Bible says, with practicality, "be filled with the Holy Spirit."

When you were converted, the Holy Spirit came into your heart, and God's Spirit witnessed with your spirit that you were a child of God. In Ephesians 1:13 it says, "Having believed, you were marked in him with a seal, the promised Holy Spirit." But it says that those same people from Ephesus needed even more; read Acts 19:1–6. "He . . . asked them, 'Did you receive the Holy Spirit when you believed?' They answered, 'No, we have not even heard that there is a Holy Spirit.' So Paul asked, 'Then what baptism did you receive?' 'John's baptism,' they replied. Paul said, 'John's baptism was a baptism of repentance. He told the people to believe in the one coming after him, that is, in Jesus.' On hearing this, they were baptized into the name of the Lord Jesus. When Paul placed his hands on them, the Holy Spirit came on them, and they spoke in tongues and prophesied."

"Thank You, Lord, that the fullness of the Spirit is for every child of God. Please show me if there is a small part of my life, or perhaps even a big part, that is not open to Your Spirit.

"Thank You that Your Holy Spirit is willing to fill my life to the fullest, just like sunlight fills a room that is open to its light. Listen, Lord, to anyone who says: 'I am throwing the curtains wide open! Fill every corner and make me like a glove that is able to do anything through Your strong hand that fills every finger.' Thank You so much. In Jesus' name, Amen."

Eleven

How Do We Receive God's Gifts?

✒

I once read a book *A Table Full of Gifts* by Annie van Essen-Bosch. Is the book a catalogue of birthday and Christmas gifts? No, she wrote about the riches described in the Bible.

We find in the Bible an abundance of riches, nourishment, peace, happiness, and answers to problems. It is so good to say, "And that is all for you. Come in and sit down and take whatever you want."

The Bible writers were sometimes at a loss in describing all those riches. They used many "un" words. "We have seen unbelievable things," "unfathomable are God's works," "unspeakable joy." When Peter uses these "un" words in 1 Peter 1:4, where he talks about the inheritance that is set aside for us and us for that inheritance, he calls that "an inheritance incorruptible and undefiled" (KJV). What a wonderful assurance—the inheritance kept for us and us for that inheritance.

How come so many words begin with "un"? The promises in the Bible are heavenly promises that we can enjoy now; but we can't describe them with earthly words. "Oh, the depth of the riches of the wisdom and knowledge of God. How unsearchable his judgments and his paths beyond tracing out!" (Rom. 11:33). We must study the Bible and discover how rich we are!

In Möttlingen, Germany, people spoke of the Bible's riches: "Nimmst's, dan hast's" (If you take it, you have it). You need to claim them. When you read a promise it is so good to say, "Thank You, Lord, that is for me!"

That claiming doesn't always happen immediately. Paul, who had so much knowledge and who knew the Lord so well, wrote in Philippians 3:12, "Not that I have already obtained all this, or have already been made perfect, but I press on to take hold of that for which Christ Jesus took hold of me." It is a battle of faith, especially in difficult circumstances, when everything is dark and threatening.

Yet it is possible. I have already mentioned my sister Betsie, who starved to death in a concentration camp. One day, when we had suffered terribly, she said, "What a wonderful day we have had. We have learned so much of the riches that we already have here on earth. And the best is yet to come, in heaven!" She really saw the embroidery of her life from God's perspective:

My life is but a weaving between my God and me,
I do not choose the colors, He works so steadily.
Oft'times He weaves in sorrow, and I in foolish pride,
Forget He sees the upper, and I the underside.

Not til the loom is silent, and the shuttles cease to fly
Will God unroll the canvas, and explain the reason why.
The dark threads are as needful in the Weaver's skillful hand,
As the threads of gold and silver in the pattern He has planned.

We see the back of the embroidery, God sees the front! He knows how beautiful it will be!

Psalm 33:20 and 21 says, "We wait in hope for the LORD; he is our help and our shield. In him our hearts rejoice, for we trust in his holy name." Perhaps you ask: "How can I do that? How can I receive these riches? I don't belong completely to the Lord and I don't understand it either." The Lord Jesus said that you have to be born again. Then you can see the kingdom of God. Being born again is being born into the family of God.

The Lord Jesus gives us new life. He makes you a child of God. On our part, we must and may receive Jesus. Just say "Yes" to the Lord Jesus. Then the Bible will become a table full of gifts!

Paul's jailer asked, "What must I do to be saved?" The answer was "Believe in the Lord Jesus Christ!" (see Acts 16:30−31). Jesus died on the cross for our sins, He became poor to make us rich. Don't overcomplicate things. Come to Jesus and say, "Will you make me, a sinner, a child of God?" If you do that, He does His part.

Let's pray. "Lord Jesus, will You, through Your Holy Spirit, show us our life from Your perspective? In heaven that will be so clear, but we need to know now. Strengthen our faith. I thank You that You do not turn away anyone who comes to You, but that You make them rich children of God. Thank You. Amen."

Twelve

Who Prepares the Table Full of Gifts for Us?

꒳

When I speak about the riches of the Gospel and the wonderful promises in the Bible, I can imagine that some will say, "Oh no, that isn't for me. That's great for my neighbor, who is so pious and the man who is so good, but I am not there yet." Let me tell you about the conditions that the Bible gives us. Jesus said, "Come to me, all you who are weary and burdened, and I will give you rest" (Matt. 11:28).

Are you weary and burdened, bound and not free? Then it is exactly you who can come to Jesus and receive rest and deliverance.

Some time ago I heard Dr. Stanley Jones speak. He was an evangelist who was then eighty-six years old. He had travelled and preached the Gospel in many different countries. It was on the final day of a conference. During the week people were asked to write down any questions—real questions with which they struggled. Dr. Jones laid his hand on the pile of paper. I thought,

"Well, it's going to take a few hours for him to answer all these questions." But something else happened. He said: "All these questions I have read, can be answered with a one-word answer, and that word is 'Jesus.' Yes, Jesus is the answer to all questions and to every need." I thought, "Is it that simple? Isn't he getting off rather lightly?" But then a ray of light entered my heart: He is right! Jesus is the answer!

Whatever the problem, the answer is the same: tell Jesus, tell it all to Him. His name is Wonderful, Counsellor, Mighty God, Eternal Father, Prince of Peace. Tell it all to Him, He is the Counsellor and He counsels!

Are you troubled by your sins? He died on the cross for your sins: read 1 John 1:7 and 9 to see what He wants to do with your sins. He wants to forgive you and cleanse you from all unrighteousness.

Do you feel lonely? He said, "And surely I am with you always, to the very end of the age" (Matt. 28:20). Perhaps you say, "It can't be that simple! Many battles must be fought and many prayers offered, before peace will come at last."

Yes, Paul too said, "I press on to take hold of that for which Christ Jesus took hold of me" (Phil. 3:12). He knew that it was there and that he only needed to take hold of it. The Lord Jesus did not need to press on to it; He had already taken hold of Paul. Therefore Paul could say, "I know whom I have believed, and am convinced that he is able to guard what I have entrusted to him for that day" (2 Tim. 1:12).

Weren't there any people whom Jesus sent away, who He was not able to help? Yes, there were the Pharisees who said, "I am good and even better than many others." If you come to Jesus in your own goodness, then you are sent away, because Jesus accepts sinners. So if you honestly mean it when you say that you are a sinner and that you have sinned, then in Jesus you will find someone who will love you and forgive you and cleanse you. First John 1:9 says, "If we confess our sins, he is faithful and just and will forgive us our sins and purify us from all unrighteousness." Perhaps someone reading says, "Yes, I did that before and experienced that happiness and forgiveness, but my life has grown so cold. When I faithfully read my Bible and had a quiet time, and went to church or to meetings, then I was rich in the Lord. But I have become so unfaithful and disobedient." Go to Jesus with that disobedience. Read Joel 2:25. It says, "I will repay you for the years the locusts have eaten." Here we read that we may return to Jesus with our backsliding and He will give us another chance.

Don't you know how to do that? He is the Good Shepherd and His sheep hear His voice. Read Psalm 23. That is all for you. Talk about it all with the Shepherd. He loves you and understands you so well.

Are you a sheep of the Good Shepherd? Do you know you are, or are you unsure? Go to Him and tell Him. Say, "Lord Jesus, I am not sure if things are right between You and me. Will You forgive my sins and cleanse me with Your blood? I accept You as my personal Savior. Thank You, Father, that I may be Your child. I so much want to have all the riches in the Bible and the wonderful promises." If you do that, He will accept you, because He said, "Whoever comes to me I will never drive away" (John 6:37).

Let's pray. "Thank You, Lord Jesus, that You love us so much that You want to be the answer to our problems. Will You show us through Your Holy Spirit just how rich we can be in You? Will You show us the sins in our lives? We want to confess them to You so that You can cleanse us. Thank You that You love sinners and that You want to change us into victorious children of God. Hallelujah, what riches. Amen."

Thirteen

Do You Long for the Table Full of Gifts?

⟫

The Bible is like a table full of gifts. Do you long for these riches? In Psalm 119:20 we read, "My soul is consumed with longing for your laws at all times." If we are consumed with longing for God's gifts, then our life will become a journey of discovery. We are assisted on that journey by the Holy Spirit who is the Owner of those riches. "The Spirit searches all things, even the deep things of God" (1 Cor. 2:10). The Bible also says "No eye has seen, no ear has heard, no mind has conceived what God has prepared for those who love him" (1 Cor. 2:9).

I read these words and said to myself, "Yes, but my love for God is so small." Then I entered and what was on the table? "God has poured out his love into our hearts by the Holy Spirit, whom he has given us" (Rom. 5:5). What abundance! I only had to open my heart and His love filled my heart and gave me love for God and for people. Do you know what I was to experience? God's love was there for deep experiences, for crises as well as for minor events and day-to-day life with the people around me. I can use the highest potential of God's love in everyday experiences. I cannot do it myself, but I don't need to. I can receive, take, get, everything I need. Take it; then you have it!

The same was true when I fought in vain against my sins. I began to analyze myself to find out where things had gone wrong. Then I read: "The Spirit searches all things"(1 Cor. 2:10). It was just like going to a doctor: you don't need to make the diagnosis yourself; the doctor does that. You just tell the doctor what you feel and where the pain is and he will figure it out. The Spirit searches all things in a similar way.

When I am on vacation, I always enjoy looking at menus posted outside restaurants. You can read what is offered and your mouth starts to water as you see all that is available!

The same delight is possible with the Lord's table full of gifts. Yes, it is possible! It is all in the Bible, where we can read all about victorious living. The Bible is God's love letter to us, and it describes the Lord Jesus, who said, "I have come that they may have life, and have it to the full" (John 10:10).

God wants to receive you and me as material in His hands, just as the potter shapes clay. This means that we must make our lives available to Him. This decision has far-reaching consequences, too far-reaching for many of us. We are interested, but it is like being in front of a beautiful shop window. We are just looking and don't intend to pay the price.

We may be pious Christians, but our ego is still on the throne. We love ourselves. The Bible says, however, "But seek first his kingdom and his righteousness, and all these things will be given to you as well" (Matt. 6:33) and "Love the Lord your God with all your heart and with all your soul and with all your mind" (Matt. 22:37). That means losing your life for Jesus' sake (see Matthew 10:39).

Following these commands means surrendering your life to Jesus. He becomes the captain of your ship. You then see everything you possess like the helmsman sees the cargo. The cargo isn't his; he has to deliver it where the owner wants it. That is not a problem, those are the captain's orders.

Our task is to hand over the whole cargo to the Owner. He who gives everything, also asks for everything! In our relationship with God we are so afraid that He will require too much of us. Therefore, we don't stretch out our hands to take. That is because we do not see reality. We need to see, but not like a mirror that reflects what is in front of it, because a mirror does not have any feeling. True sight comes forth out of life, and influences life. It is the Holy Spirit who opens our eyes.

Be filled with God's Spirit! Then you will see what abundance there is, and how safe we can be. It means keeping your life by being willing to lose it.

Let's pray. "Thank You, Lord, that You want everything from us in order to give us everything. Thank You, Holy Spirit, that You open our eyes, so that we can see how rich we are in the Lord. Thank You, Lord Jesus, that You accomplished everything on the cross, and that You became poor to make us so rich. Hallelujah, what a Savior! Amen."

Fourteen

How Can We Get to the Table Full of Gifts?

꓿

The Bible describes an abundance of riches: peace that passes all understanding, forgiveness, love, everything in abundance. Why is that for you? Because your heavenly Father knows that you need these things (see Matthew 6:32). God's gifts are not forced upon us: we may receive them with joy and gratitude. God's love does not force anything upon us and it can wait until we stretch out our hands for Him to fill.

We have to be careful that we don't just admire the Bible's promises. We can be just like people standing in front of a beautiful shop window, who don't go in because they aren't willing to pay the price. A price must be paid for the table of riches. Here we see that on our part it is not striving, battling, or trying but a surrender of our lives into the hand of the Lord.

The Lord wants to prepare us for His return. Everything we need is on the table. In 1 Thessalonians 5:23 it says, "May God himself, the God of peace, sanctify you through and through.

May your whole spirit, soul and body be kept blameless at the coming of our Lord Jesus Christ." Is that possible? Yes, because Paul then says, "The one who calls you is faithful and he will do it" (1 Thess. 5:24).

The most important thing for a Christian in these times is to be ready for Jesus' return. The signs of the end of the age are so clearly visible that we can expect Him soon. It gives us courage and comfort to read in the Bible that the Lord Himself wants to prepare us. The bride is being prepared to meet the groom.

In Philippians 1:6, Paul says, "Being confident of this, that he who began a good work in you will carry it on to completion until the day of Christ Jesus." On the cross everything necessary was accomplished.

The Lord expects complete surrender from us. The potter can't shape clay that is not completely in his hands. Complete surrender means making our life available to God. God wants our lives in His hands, like a potter shapes the clay. If we reject God's desire as too extreme, then we are just "interested," like the window-shopper who doesn't want to pay the price. Our interest soon passes away.

No person is complete by himself. Something has to be added to make life worth living. We are all looking for that "something." There is an emptiness to be filled. We often accept less than top-quality filling. We must seek truly great content so that all parts of our being are filled.

The Lord Jesus says, "I have come that they may have life, and have it to the full" (John 10:10). With these words Jesus provides an answer to our need. He offers us a life of abundance. He wants to enter into a covenant with you. That demands complete commitment from both parties.

The result is a new person—you in the Lord, He in you. Then we can rejoice in our redemption, because we no longer stand there as sinners. Because "God made him who had no sin to be sin for us, so that in him we might become the righteousness of God" (2 Cor. 5:21). We become a new creation.

Often the "old being" still wants to have its say. In Ephesians 6 it says that we need the armor of God. We need that to the very end. But we are standing on victory ground!

Are you worrying about your sins? We need to discern who is showing us our sins. The devil is an accuser of the children of God. He has a full-time job. Day and night he comes with his reproaches. When he has the chance, the accuser says, "There is no hope for you; you aren't good enough." But when the Holy Spirit shows us our sins, it is always in the light of the finished work of the cross. He says to us, "Jesus died on the cross for the sins which now weigh so heavily upon you." The prophet Isaiah says, "But he was pierced for our transgressions, he was crushed for our iniquities; the punishment that brought us peace was upon him" (Isa. 53:5).

Read Romans 8:31–34: "What, then, shall we say in response to this? If God is for us, who can be against us? He who did not spare his own Son, but gave him up for us all—how will he not also, along with him, graciously give us all things? Who will bring any charge against those whom God has chosen? It is God who justifies. Who is he that condemns? Christ Jesus, who died—more than that, who was raised to life—is at the right hand of God and is also interceding for us." For children of God worried about their sins, a table full of gifts is described there.

What exactly is surrender? We know that we may not compromise. It is not a question of feeling but of the will. In her book, *A Table Full of Gifts*, Annie van Essen-Bosch writes of how we can only really receive God's gifts if we bring our sins and problems to the Lord. Then there is room for what God wants to give us. If pride, resentment, hard-heartedness, and all our burdens are brought to the Lord, indeed our whole life, then He can richly give that life back to us. Then we are no longer owners, but stewards. We can feel so rich and joyful if we give Him, the Creator, the ownership of our life.

I saw such a good example of surrender in my father. He sometimes said, "My name is on my watchmaker's shop but actually God's name should be on it. Because I am a watchmaker by the grace of God." He knew what surrender meant, and how we can be stewards.

Let's pray. "Lord, will You prepare us for Your return? I give myself completely to You, so that You, who began a good work in me, may carry it on to completion until the day of Christ Jesus. Hallelujah. Amen."

Fifteen

A New Creation

Therefore, if anyone is in Christ, he is a new creation.
—2 CORINTHIANS 5:17

If we meet the Lord Jesus, it isn't a question of half measures. We don't get anywhere by patching things up; that's unnecessary. When He renews and redeems us, it isn't like a flag that flies on a ramshackle house. It is a completely new house. The Lord Jesus gives us the right to be children of God, a new creation, sanctified and holy.

You may say, "Wait a minute; it can't happen just like that. Aren't we inclined toward evil, unable to do anything good?" That's true. But Christ makes us a new creation! It is very healthy and necessary to be aware of your sins, to discover them. But it is one of the devil's tricks that he makes us think that it is particularly pious if we go about weighed down deeply by our sins. The awareness of sin is a needed, transitory phase in your spiritual life. The devil tries to make it the center—a pitfall with steep sides. Yes, our sins may be many, but on the cross everything necessary to redeem us was accomplished.

There is life and salvation in looking to the cross. If we look to the Lord Jesus we forget everything else. The wonderful appearance of His being is the hour of the birth of our new self. Our new eyes must start to see other things. Our new heart has to beat and it has a different rhythm!

Paul calls us saints and the family of God, and as if that weren't enough, a temple of the Holy Spirit. You may say, "That's possible for a mature Christian, a child of God beyond reproach. Yes, they can be temples of God's Spirit. But me . . . ?"

Let's see what the Bible says in Isaiah 57:15: "For this is what the high and lofty One says—he who lives forever, whose name is holy: I live in a high and holy place, but also with him who is contrite and lowly in spirit, to revive the spirit of the lowly and to revive the heart of the contrite." John says, "If anyone acknowledges that Jesus is the Son of God, God lives in him and he in God" (1 John 4:15). In Revelation 3:20 we read that the Lord Jesus Himself takes the initiative: "Here I am! I stand at the door and knock. If anyone hears my voice and opens the door, I will come in and eat with him, and he with me." He is going to dwell within us and we can be sure that He will hold a great spring cleaning. He makes us new people, a new creation. Perhaps you say, "But is it really that simple?" Yes, it is very drastic, but also very simple.

I once visited a prison in Germany. I spoke to a man in his cell and he came to the Lord through the text Revelation 3:20. The pastor came in later and I said, "Tell the pastor what happened." The man started out on a long story about a spiritual discussion with me, a new vision, and a long, complicated tale. I interrupted him and said, "Stop. Just tell him what happened. Someone knocked. Who was that?" He immediately said: "Jesus." "Someone opened. Who was that?" "Me." Suddenly he saw how simple it was and how real. The next day I heard him give a clear testimony during a meeting full of ex-prisoners.

Did you hear it? Someone is knocking. Who is that person? Jesus. Someone has to open the door; who is that person? You. Will you do it?

"Thank You, Lord Jesus, that You came in and made me a new creation. Thank You for the big spring cleaning, for Your blood that cleanses us from all sin. Thank You that You will now really come and live in the heart of anyone who says, 'Jesus knocked. I said "Yes,"' and that You make them a new person, a new creation. Hallelujah. Amen."

Sixteen

Have You Been Born Again?

⤳

The Lord Jesus once said, "You should not be surprised at my saying, 'You must be born again'" (John 3:7).

The question I am going to ask you is, have you been born again? You may read these meditations regularly; you may perhaps read your Bible, go to church, and pray. But have you been born again?

In Revelation 3 you can read about people in Laodicea who were quite religious. If you were to ask them, "How are things going for you spiritually?" they would say: "We are rich, very rich, and we have no need of anything." But there was something very important missing. The Lord Jesus stood outside the door of their hearts and He was knocking on their hearts. He said: "If anyone hears my voice and opens the door, I will come in and eat with him, and he with me" (Rev. 3:20).

You see, if you have not yet been made completely new, then really the answer is to be born again. Is it that simple? Yes. If Jesus comes into your heart He will perform that miracle. You will be born into the family of God. Jesus said, "You should not be surprised at my saying, 'You must be born again.'"(John 3:7). It is the obligatory way, the way you must go. Of course, Jesus performs the miracle of rebirth, but you have to come—you must come. Is that what you want? If so, what do you have to do? Jesus is knocking and you have to let Him in now. What happens when Jesus comes into your heart? He sees your sins; and you suddenly see them very clearly too. There is no other way.

The wonderful thing is that you now know what you must do about your sins—confess them. "If we confess our sins, he is faithful and just and will forgive us our sins and purify us from all unrighteousness" (1 John 1:9). The blood of Jesus cleanses us. Jesus starts working in your heart. He washes away the sins you confess. Is that all as far as sins are concerned? No, it isn't just confessing them, it is also turning away from them. But you are no longer on your own. Together with Jesus you wage war against sin.

You cannot do it alone, but He can do it. He puts the Holy Spirit in your heart and that brings the fruit of the Spirit (see Galatians 5:22): love, joy, peace, patience, kindness. . . . The Bible suddenly becomes very different; it becomes a love letter from God. If you ask Jesus to come into your heart, then He comes and His Spirit confesses with your spirit that you are a child of God. You start to understand the Bible and it makes you extremely joyful, because you see the answer to your problems, the biggest problems in your life.

Everyone has at least two big problems: the problem of sin and the problem of death, and they are answered. You see, Jesus carried the sin of the whole world on the cross, including your sins. He accomplished everything there. He suffered terribly, He was in awful pain, but He wanted to do that out of love, to pay for our sins.

We are also strengthened in our struggle against sin. You are redeemed and you are also victorious over your sins in Jesus. Coming to Jesus is just a beginning. The birth of a child is a start, and being born again is also a beginning. It is the start of a life glorifying God—a victorious life, a life strong through the redemption, help, and presence of the Lord Jesus.

Have you not been born again? Come to Jesus then! What do you have to do? Speak to Him, very simply. He has knocked on the door of your heart and you heard it today; and now He is waiting. The Lord Jesus is gentle; He doesn't force down the door of your heart. You have to open it, and if you really mean it when you say, "Yes, Lord Jesus," then He will come in. In John 1:12 it says, "Yet to all who received him, to those who believed in his name, he gave the right to become children of God." Then you are a child of God. Will you let Him in?

Let's pray. "Lord Jesus, will You make the way clear for him, for her, who is now making a decision for You. Will You remove all resistance, all doubt, all 'yes, buts' and also all the devils and demons because they don't want them to do it; but I thank You that You will send those demons away. Make the path clear between You and him or her. Thank You, Lord. Thank You."

Now we will be quiet for a moment, and you can give your answer to the Lord.

"Thank You, that he or she can now say: 'Yes, Lord Jesus, come into my heart, make me a child of God, perform that great miracle in me of being born again into Your family.' Thank You, Lord Jesus. Amen."

Now you must speak to the Lord some more. You belong to Him. He hears everything you say and He loves you so very much!

Seventeen

A Very Important Decision

⤳

There was once a jailer in a prison in Philippi who asked a question you, too, along with many other people, might share. He asked Paul (Acts 16:30–31), "Sirs, what must I do to be saved?" Paul answered with a very short sentence: "Believe in the Lord Jesus, and you will be saved—you and your household." Is it really that simple?

I remember a conversation I had with a doctor in New Zealand. I had spoken to him for a whole day about conversion and what he had to do, but he didn't want to make a decision for the Lord Jesus. There came a moment when I said to him, "Accept Jesus, believe and trust in Him and you will be saved." He was suddenly able to do it and he said, "Yes, Lord Jesus, I believe in You. Thank You for rescuing me and that I am now saved." Do you know what I wondered when he said that so simply? "Is it really so simple and easy?" Yes, it is that easy; it is that simple. That is to say, it wasn't at all easy for the Lord Jesus to make it possible. It was a terrible, heavy cross that He had to bear, and on which He died after suffering terribly. But He did everything necessary for us to be saved.

Now, on our part, we need to stretch out our hands. You see, if I want to give you something you have to stretch out your hand so that I can put it in it. It is just like that with salvation. You have to stretch out your hands and then Jesus lays salvation in them. It is saying "Yes" to Jesus. Nothing else? Well yes, there is more, but that will come later. The big decision, that "Yes," is the most important.

I once asked a woman: "Would you like to accept the Lord Jesus?" She responded, "Oh, I have prayed so much in my life, and the Lord heard my prayers and I know that He blessed me so much. He helped me when life was terribly difficult." Then I said to her: "Look, if a boy asks a girl to marry him and she says: 'You have helped me so much, you have been so kind to me, we have had such good conversations, I am so happy that you have always been so good to me,' then the boy would say, 'Yes, that is all well and good, but we aren't talking about that now. I want you to say "Yes" because I love you.' All being well, she won't think of all that has happened, but she will say 'Yes!' That short, decisive word means great joy for them both, but it is just the beginning."

You may have already experienced much with the Lord. You already love Him, and you know that He loves you. You have prayed a lot, and many prayers have been answered, but the Lord Jesus loves you so much that He is not satisfied with anything less than having your heart, your love. If you say: "Yes, Lord Jesus, I accept Your salvation, I want to belong to You," then He will save you for all eternity. Then you belong together, Jesus and you. That is a wonderful start, just as a "Yes" from a girl to a boy is also a beginning. This, however, is much bigger, because Jesus gives you eternal life. He gives you an answer to the problem of your sin. He makes you a member of God's family. The Bible becomes a love letter from God to you—all because you have now accepted Jesus. He will fill your heart with His Holy Spirit and its fruit—love, joy, peace, and much more. Will you say "Yes" to Him? Don't look at everything you have already experienced—either difficult or wonderful. Simply realize that Jesus is here. He loves you and He wants to take you in His arms. He wants to make you happy and give you eternal life. He wants to give you a victorious life now, He wants to give you His Spirit. He has asked you. What is your answer?

Let's pray. "Lord Jesus, I thank You that You love her and love him so much. Thank You for being so happy when he or she says 'Yes,' and that You will then save them. Did You hear who said this, Lord? Yes, of course You heard whoever said: 'Yes, Jesus.' You didn't just hear it, but You are happy about it. Lord, did You see the people, did You see that one there, who really wanted to do it, but didn't? You know why. There was a 'Yes, but' and that is the very opposite of 'Yes.' Oh, Lord Jesus, will You take away the 'Yes, but'? Will You take away the whispering of the enemy who says that it can't be that quick, that it isn't that easy. Make the way free between Yourself and him or her.

"Thank You that the path is now free of obstacles. Lord, You have heard him or her who also said: 'Yes, Jesus, I mean it.' Thank You, Jesus, that You now lay Your hand on their lives and that You will bring her and him in, and that You have saved them. Thank You, Lord Jesus. What love! Hallelujah. Amen."

Eighteen

In Black and White

*For if you forgive men when they sin against you, your heavenly
Father will also forgive you. But if you do not forgive men their
sins, your Father will not forgive your sins.*

—MATTHEW 6:14–15

We read the signs of Jesus' return in both the Bible and
the newspapers. The Bible says in Mark 13:35 and
1 John 3:3, "Therefore keep watch" and "Everyone who has this
hope in him purifies himself, just as he is pure." Well, the signs
are clear. The continual rumors of war, people consumed with
fear and anxiety about the world's future, Israel back in its own
country, increasing persecution of Jews and Christians, and the
rise in spiritism.

Let's consider this: if Jesus were to return today, would you
be ready? Are you one of the wise or foolish virgins in the
parable in Matthew 25:1–13? Are you a bride with a heart full
of love for the Bridegroom and full of longing for His return?

Paul warns us so clearly in 2 Corinthians 5:20, "We are therefore Christ's ambassadors, as though God were making his appeal through us. We implore you on Christ's behalf: Be reconciled to God." You are not reconciled to God if you are unreconciled with your fellow human beings. I once had a disagreement with some Christian colleagues. They did something unpleasant toward me. I was angry, but I brought it to the Lord. He forgave my anger, cleansed my heart with His blood, and I forgave them. Or so I thought.

Then a good friend told me, "Your friends aren't at all concerned about what happened. They simply say that they didn't do it." I replied, "That's easy for them to say, but I have it in black and white." "Oh," my friend answered, "in black and white? Tell me, where are your past sins? You, yourself, told me that they have been thrown into the depths of the sea, and there is a sign: 'No fishing.' As far as the west is from the east so far has he removed our transgressions from us. The Lord even says in Isaiah 44:22, 'I have swept away your offenses like a cloud, your sins like the morning mist.' Your sins are gone, but you still have their sins in black and white?"

I was shocked. I collected all the letters from these friends and burned them. It was a sweet fragrance to the Lord. I felt so happy. The Lord Jesus says in His warning in Luke 21:36, "Be always on the watch, and pray that you may be able to escape all that is about to happen, and that you may be able to stand before the Son of Man." I know that neither you nor I will be able to do that if we still keep the sins of others in black and white. Jesus could very well return today. Don't go to sleep before all that black and white is burned.

In his book *Sit Walk Stand*, Watchman Nee explains very clearly how it is really possible for a child of God to forgive once you realize who you are in Christ Jesus. When the Lord died on the cross, He did not just carry your sins away but also your old self was crucified with Him. And so the unforgiving you, who finds it impossible to forgive, has been crucified and completely taken away.

God dealt with the whole situation on the cross; there is nothing left for you to settle. Just say to Him, "Lord, I cannot forgive and I will no longer try to do it; but I trust that You in me will do it. I can't forgive and love, but I trust that You will forgive and love in my place and that You will do these things in me." God is so rich that it is His greatest joy to forgive. His treasure stores are so full that it grieves Him when we refuse to allow Him to richly lavish these treasures upon us.

Paul says in Colossians 3:12–15, "Therefore, as God's chosen people, holy and dearly loved, clothe yourselves with compassion, kindness, humility, gentleness and patience. Bear with each other and forgive whatever grievances you may have against one another. Forgive as the Lord forgave you. And over all these virtues put on love, which binds them all together in perfect unity. Let the peace of Christ rule in your hearts, since as members of one body you were called to peace. And be thankful." This text is a diving board. We need to plunge into the ocean of God's love. We must take a running jump, a deep dive, into that ocean, throwing ourselves into the lake of His love. Have you taken a running jump today?

In Romans 5:5 it says that the love of God has been poured out into our hearts by the Holy Spirit who has been given to us. If you throw an open bottle into the sea, it immediately fills with water. So, too, by complete surrender into the hands of our Savior, we are filled and surrounded by the ocean of God's love. Just what we need and so overwhelmingly wonderful! "If

I speak in the tongues of men and of angels, but have not love.
... If I have the gift of prophecy and can fathom all mysteries
and all knowledge, and if I have faith that can move mountains,
but have not love, I am nothing" (1 Cor. 13:1–2).

Have you ever doubted your love for the Lord and your
love for your enemies? I did. Have you ever doubted the love
of God for His Son Jesus? Never, never. Do you know that
Jesus welcomes you in that love? Take the plunge!

"May God himself, the God of peace, sanctify you through
and through. May your whole spirit, soul and body be kept
blameless at the coming of our Lord Jesus Christ. The one who
calls you is faithful and he will do it" (1 Thess. 5:23–24).

"Lord Jesus, show us all where we have kept records in black
and white of other people's sins. Our love, our power, is too
small; but Your love and power wants to burn the accounts
today. In that way You are preparing us for Your return. Thank
You that You who began a good work in us will carry it on to
completion until Your day, the day of Your return. Hallelujah.
Amen."

Nineteen

A Few Thoughts on Guidance

꒦

We were sitting with a group of boys and girls around a campfire. The campers had asked me to talk about my travels around the world.

I told them how the Lord had said, "Go to Japan." I had arrived in Japan, not knowing a single word of Japanese. I, nevertheless, obeyed and the Lord opened many doors for me. I was able to work in the largest prisons in Japan.

A boy interrupted me: "I don't get that at all, when you say 'the Lord said.' Explain HOW the Lord said that. Did you hear a voice, or did you sense something in your thoughts, or in your heart? You said yesterday that it was important to know the will of God. I don't want to argue with you, but I really want to know. What does God want and how does He show us His will? I can't figure it out. How do you do know?"

"Thank you for this question. We all struggle with it, sooner or later, as we seek to walk with the Lord. I believe it is one of the most important things in our lives as Christians. Knowing the will of God should be the number one prayer request both for yourself and in your intercessions for others. You often arrive at a crossroads in life, and you must know which path to take. You feel so safe if someone who knows the way will be your guide."

First, we need to find out what the Bible says about guidance. I remember the Bible text my mother and father were given on the occasion of their marriage. It hung in our living room when I was young. "I will instruct you and teach you in the way you should go; I will counsel you and watch over you" (Ps. 32:8). John writes, "We know also that the Son of God has come and has given us understanding, so that we may know him who is true. And we are in him who is true—even in his Son Jesus Christ. He is the true God and eternal life" (1 John 5:20). Jesus Himself said, "But when he, the Spirit of truth, comes, he will guide you into all truth" (John 16:13).

No one gets lost on a straight path. All the promises in the Bible are in Jesus: Yes and Amen (see 2 Corinthians 1:20). That means that they are there for you and for me—whether you have known the Lord for a long time, or only accepted the Lord Jesus today or have yet to accept Him as Savior and Lord. You see, it is just a beginning.

All the riches described in the Bible are your possession. It is a like a checkbook. The checks are in your name and have been signed by Jesus. Now you have to cash the checks. The devil says that the Bible's bank account has been frozen, but that is a lie. That is why you must read the Bible as a love letter from God. For every promise you read, say: "Thank You." Say "Thank You," too, for the promise of Psalm 32:8, "I will instruct you and teach you in the way you should go; I will counsel you and watch over you."

One of the most important tasks is to know God's will. We Christians are often much too busy with unimportant things. If you do not know the will of the Lord, you must put everything aside and concentrate on finding out which path is right. There was once a country with a port that was very dangerous. Under the surface of the water there were many rocks. Now there were clear markers, but you couldn't see them at night. So the people set up six beacons, three on the left and three on the right. If the lights formed two straight lines, then the helmsman knew that his course was safe. God gives His guidance in three ways. If these three are in agreement, then you know that you are safe:

1. Prayer
2. God's Word, the Bible
3. Circumstances

If you know God's hidden companionship, your prayer will become a conversation instead of a soliloquy. Here is an exercise that you could call keeping "my eyes . . . ever on the LORD, for only he will release my feet from the snare" (Ps. 25:15). You learn to recognize God's voice. Job says, "Submit to God and be at peace with him" (Job 22:21). But verse 22 is also true: "Accept instruction from his mouth and lay up his words in your heart." You have to be prepared to obey Him.

Just after the war, I had a very clear experience. I said, "I will work wherever God leads me, but the one country I never want to go to is Germany." After that when I asked for guidance, I received absolutely none. I didn't know what was wrong, but I understood that there must be disobedience somewhere. You see, it is so good to go to the Boss immediately to consult Him. I asked the Lord, "Is there disobedience somewhere?" The answer came immediately: "Germany." "Then I will go to Germany too," I replied and contact was restored.

In my books you may read that the Lord used me more in Germany than in any other country. The German people aren't my enemies. My greatest friends live there, but there had been enemies too. Even the fact of those former enemies became a wonderful experience. When Jesus tells you to love your enemies, He gives you the love that He asks of you.

Make a game of asking for God's guidance so you will practice it:

- ask for it;
- really want it, long for it;
- if you get it, accept it.

As you seek God's guidance you discover that God takes the initiative in your life. He will redirect you if you start out on the wrong path. The Good Shepherd finds it so important that you do His will, that if one sheep strays, He will willingly leave ninety-nine at home and look for the lost one.

The first step is to ask Jesus to be your Lord. If you go on a train journey, you first find out which train you need to take. If you are on the right train, you don't need to worry about red and green lights; the engineer takes care of that. If you need to change trains, the conductor tells you when. The Lord Jesus is the engineer. Place your trust in Him. The Holy Spirit is the conductor; obey His leading! You will know whether you are being guided by Him, because, when you are, you experience peace that passes all understanding. The enemy can imitate a lot, but not God's peace. To receive God's peace, you have to be at peace with Him and that is possible if you open your heart to Jesus. "Here I am! I stand at the door and knock. If anyone hears my voice and opens the door, I will come in and eat with him, and he with me" (Rev. 3:20).

"Thank You Lord, for being such a good Shepherd. Thank You that You lead Your sheep safely. I place my hand in Yours and together—You and I—we push onwards. What a safe way that is. Amen."

Twenty

Jesus, the Messiah

ϗ

Today I want to speak to Jews and those who love them, for they can then pass on this message.

In 1844 there was a watchmaker in Haarlem who received a visit from Pastor Witteveen. They discussed the needs of Jerusalem and they both decided to start a weekly prayer meeting in their respective neighborhoods where Christians could pray for the peace of Jerusalem and blessings for the Jews. My grandfather (for he was that watchmaker!) started that prayer meeting in his watchmaker's workshop. The prayer meeting was so remarkable in that period that my father, who told me about it, knew the year it had started. Christians now frequently pray for Jews, but it was not so common then.

A hundred years later my grandfather's son and many grandchildren were arrested in that same house, because they had saved Jews. The majority of them died in prison. Such was the incomprehensible but divine answer to my grandfather's prayers. During the German occupation from 1940–1945, we did everything we could to save Jews from Adolf Hitler's terrible plans. Friends often warned us. They said, especially to our father, "You will end up in jail if you always have Jews in the house. Stop that dangerous work." Father then answered, "I am too old for life in prison, but it will be an honor to give my life for God's holy people, Israel." He spoke truly. Ten days after Father was taken to Scheveningen jail, he died.

Jesus, the Messiah, will return again. One of the most obvious signs of the Messiah's imminent return is the return of the Jews to their country (see Isaiah 66:8, 20, 22). One of the most important moments in the history of our times was May 10, 1948. Rees Howells, who had great love for the people of Israel for whom he seriously and faithfully prayed, said, "The rebirth of the state of Israel is the greatest act of God in 2000 years." God is working in the hearts of present-day Jews to prepare them for the Messiah's return. A rabbi who studied Isaiah seriously and with faith came to the conclusion that two Messiahs must come, the suffering servant of the Lord of Isaiah 53 (Ben Joseph), the other one the coming King of Isaiah 66 (Ben David). We, who have both the Old and New Testaments, know that there is only one Messiah: Jesus, who first came as a suffering servant of the Lord, who bore the sins of the whole world when He died on the cross, and who will return as the King of Kings. Every knee shall bow to Him (Phil. 2:10) and every tongue shall confess Him. Then He will bring about the kingdom of God on this earth, and the prayer that has been prayed by so many millions in the Lord's Prayer, "Your will be done on earth as it is in heaven," will be answered.

The Jews are God's ancient people. They too shall see Jesus. The prophet has already said, "They will look on me, the one they have pierced" (Zech. 12:10). There is no political answer to the needs of this age. The scholars claim that there is no hope, that the world can perhaps exist for another thirty years, but then the end will come. The greatest and most wonderful answer is that the Messiah will return and make all things new. Then the earth will be full of the knowledge of the Lord as the waters cover the sea. Right now the earth is full of crime, pollution, hatred, and disasters. But there is hope; there is a future for the world. The best is yet to come! Whenever you see the great needs of the world, pray: Come, Lord Jesus, come quickly. "The Spirit and the bride say, 'Come!' And let him who hears say, 'Come!' Whoever is thirsty, let him come; and whoever wishes, let him take the free gift of the water of life" (Rev. 22:17).

The Lord in heaven is not surprised at what is happening now. In the Bible it says that whoever is vile will get viler, whoever is pure, purer (see Revelation 22:11). Everything is heading toward a climax. In the Old Testament we read, "And afterward, I will pour out my Spirit on all people. Your sons and daughters will prophesy, your old men will dream dreams, your young men will see visions. Even on my servants, both men and women, I will pour out my Spirit in those days" (Joel 2:28–29). We see that happening now. So many young people are being filled with the Holy Spirit, and also many Jews.

So many Christians prayed and fasted during the Six Day War in Israel in 1967. I believe in the blessing of Abraham for people and nations: "I will bless those who bless you, and whoever curses you I will curse" (Gen. 12:3). Nations are also being blessed; the peoples who are prepared to stand up for the Jews can expect a blessing from God. That I, an eighty-year-old, may still do such wonderful work is such an unusual blessing. Very few my age are still able to work like this. I sometimes ask myself if this is the blessing given to me by the Lord because my family and I dedicated our lives to saving Jews, and four of us died. Whoever wants to be ready for the return of the Messiah must be in a right relationship with God and other people. "Everyone who has this hope in him purifies himself, just as he is pure" (1 John 3:3). This is possible because if we surrender to the Messiah, Jesus, He who began a good work in us will carry it on to completion until the day of Christ Jesus (see Philippians 1:6). The Messiah longs for us more than we long for Him. What assurance! Working for Him is not the most important thing, but people are the most important. There are so many Christians who feel united with Israel. We believe in the Old Testament and often understand more of it than the Jews do, precisely because we have the New Testament. There, in the Revelation of John, we read not only about the antichrist but also: "Do not harm the land or the sea or the trees until we put a seal on the foreheads of the servants of our God" (Rev. 7:3). In Revelation 9:4 it says that the locusts will only harm people who do not have the seal of God on their foreheads; and in Revelation 19:20–21 we read how the army of the King of Kings battled against those who received the mark of the beast.

Present-day man needs vision and insight. The Bible clearly reveals God's plan. After the crisis of the battle between Christ and the antichrist comes the wonderful future of the earth, when the Messiah will reign.

"Lord, we pray for the peace of Jerusalem and the salvation of the Jews. Preserve and protect them. They are so often in such great danger. Open the eyes of Your children for the blessing that You give them—You who bless those who bless Abraham and curse those who curse him. Guide us in Your truth, Lord. In Jesus' name. Amen."

Twenty-One

In Training for the Final Battle

Dear Father, in Jesus' name we pray that through this message today, You will allow us to understand better what it means to be prepared for Jesus' return. Amen.

In Philippians 2:9–11 it says, "Therefore God exalted him to the highest place and gave him the name that is above every name, that at the name of Jesus every knee should bow, in heaven and on earth and under the earth, and every tongue confess that Jesus Christ is Lord, to the glory of God the Father."

Yes, that is the final certain victory. It will be extremely important whether you and I then bow before the Lord as our Savior and Redeemer, or as our Judge.

There is a great battle being fought in the invisible realms in the whole world. The battle keeps increasing. Ernst Maning once said, "We have reached an hour in the history of our civilization, which we could call the most serious crisis man has ever experienced." This is not something that only Christians see; the whole world knows that we are living in appalling times. But God's logistics are perfect. *Logistics* is a military word that means, among other things, "provisions." God is a general who knows exactly where and how the battle must be fought and where defense is needed. In the end there will be a tremendous battle.

One of the first conditions for battle is that we have to know our enemy; his strengths and his weaknesses. "Be self-controlled and alert. Your enemy, the devil, prowls around like a roaring lion looking for someone to devour" (1 Peter 5:8).

The children of God around the whole world know that we are in training for the final battle. These people often go through difficult times. It is so wonderful to know that the final battle will reach its climax in the victory that we read about just now in Philippians: every knee shall bow before Jesus. But all those living in the time of the final battle will not be the only ones to take part in it. For us, too, everyday life is a battlefield: the training field. We need the armor of God that we read about in Ephesians 6, not only in the future, but also now. We all have to put that armor on because we are not fighting against flesh and blood, but against the spiritual forces of evil in the heavenly realms.

It is possible for all of us to be more than conquerors now, and that is because we do not need to fight in our own strength, but through total surrender. Paul says, "I know whom I have believed, and am convinced that he is able to guard what I have entrusted to him for that day" (2 Tim. 1:12)—the day of Christ Jesus. If we surrender completely to that strong hand, we will be conquerors.

We ourselves cannot be strong in this battle. We cannot win the final battle. But Jesus is Victor. If we place our weak hand in the strong hand of Him who has all power in heaven and on earth, He will make us more than conquerors. Yes, then we can say, "He will keep you strong to the end, so that you will be blameless on the day of our Lord Jesus Christ" (1 Cor. 1:8). You and I blameless? Yes, that is possible—not in our own strength but through Jesus.

"Oh, Lord Jesus, I thank You that even if I am weak, I can be strong in You. Thank You that Your power is made perfect in our weakness. Lord, listen to whoever now says, 'I cannot do it, but I place my weak hand in Your strong hand'—and You will do it. Hallelujah! What a Savior! Oh Lord Jesus, come quickly and make me prepared. Amen."

Twenty-Two

Preparation

Thank You, Lord Jesus, that You warned us about these days shortly before Your return. Thank You for instructing us in Your Word to be ready. Will You use the words in this message to help us be more prepared, yes, completely prepared for Your coming? Prepare me, Lord, prepare me to stand before Your throne. Amen.

Our whole life is a preparation for eternity; we know that. But we don't realize it very often. These days, it is much easier to imagine that Jesus could return at any moment. All the certainties of daily life have disappeared. It is so marvelous to have security in Jesus.

The Lord Jesus spoke about His second coming: "As it was in the days of Noah, so it will be at the coming of the Son of Man. For in the days before the flood, people were eating and drinking, marrying and giving in marriage, up to the day Noah entered the ark; and they knew nothing about what would happen until the flood came and took them all away. That is how it will be at the coming of the Son of Man. . . . Therefore keep watch, because you do not know on what day your Lord will come" (Matt. 24:37–39, 42). And in Luke 21:34 it says, "Be careful, or your hearts will be weighed down with dissipation, drunkenness and the anxieties of life, and that day will close on you unexpectedly like a trap." Yes, when Jesus comes it will be like the days of Noah.

I am about to set off on a journey to Israel, Vietnam, and Indonesia. I still listen to the news, play the piano, and enjoy tasty desserts. But my suitcase is packed and I have a passport and travelers' checks in my purse. I am also deciding which vegetables we need to buy today and whether we will need milk. Noah's wife might also have cooked in the small kitchen on the ark the day before the Lord closed the door from the outside. But she didn't forget that there would be a flood and she must have been greatly relieved that her family was prepared for it.

Part of the planning for battle is deciding where it will be fought. For you and me that place is everyday life, our kitchen, school, university, hospital, or business. My father was a watchmaker and he was definitely concerned about providing for our daily needs. But in all of this, he was hidden with Jesus in God.

The Lord Jesus himself said that in John 15—as the vines and the branches are linked together, the one in the other, so must you be in Him and He in you. If we have the assurance that we are in Him, then there is no danger that the day of the Lord will close in upon us like a trap. When Father was taken away to the jail in which he died ten days later, he said to me: "The best is yet to come." The way to be prepared is to surrender to Him.

In 1 Thessalonians 5:23–24 it says, "May God himself, the God of peace, sanctify you through and through. May your whole spirit, soul and body be kept blameless at the coming of our Lord Jesus Christ. The one who calls you is faithful and he will do it."

Just imagine it: you and I, blameless! No, we can't do that; it is only possible if we put our weak hand into the strong hand of the Lord." Being confident of this, that he who began a good work in you will carry it on to completion until the day of Christ Jesus" (Phil. 1:6).

I once asked a businessman if he had surrendered completely to the Lord, and he said: "No, because I am way too busy to do that. I am up to my ears in work." Then I replied, "You are just like a mountain climber who has hired a guide, and he gets to a place where it is very steep and terribly difficult to climb. The guide says: 'Let me help!' but the man says, 'Don't you see how steep it is here, how hard this mountain is to climb? Do you think I have time now for a guide?'"

It is especially when we are up to our ears in work that we need a guide. The Lord Jesus is our guide. We need Him especially when we are overwhelmed with the concerns and hectic pace of everyday life. Surrender to Him. He will make you more than a conqueror, and if you surrender to Him completely, He will hold on to you to the end and nothing, absolutely nothing, can separate us from the love of God in Christ Jesus.

"Thank You, Lord, that You are conqueror and that You want to make us more than conquerors. Lord, listen to those who have read this message, and who say, 'Yes, Lord, I give myself completely to You. I cannot do it, but You can. Lord Jesus, hold me close to Your heart. I want to be with You, hidden with You in God.' It can't be safer than that. Thank You, Lord, that You love us that much. Hallelujah. Amen."

Twenty-Three

Prepared for Jesus' Return

In Luke 21:36 we read, "Be always on the watch, and pray that you may be able to escape all that is about to happen, and that you may be able to stand before the Son of Man."

I am going to tell you something wonderful today. You, yes, you! can be ready, even if Jesus should return today. How can that be? We can read the answer in the Bible. I know very well that many Dutch people have said, "Oh, come on, Johannes de Heer [a well-known Dutch preacher] believed that Jesus would return soon, but he didn't live to see it! Peter said that since the fathers died everything goes on as it has since the beginning of creation. So why should we believe that before our time?"

Look, Jesus said that we have to take note of the signs of the times, and if you reason like that you are a "sign of the times" yourself. Listen to this in 2 Peter 3:3–4: "First of all, you must understand that in the last days scoffers will come, scoffing and following their own evil desires. They will say, 'Where is this "coming" he promised? Ever since our fathers died, everything goes on as it has since the beginning of creation.'" Can you see that you are a sign? A sign that we are in the last days? Because, in that case, you are a scoffer. I am afraid that you are following your own cravings if you talk like that. Of course you don't want to do that, because when we one day stand before the Son of Man, our own cravings will be stumbling blocks to us.

Perhaps you say that you aren't ready yet. You will understand, of course, that Jesus is not going to wait until everyone is ready. He is coming and there will be a time when everyone will bow down before Him, both those who are ready and those who aren't. Then the question will be whether you will bend your knees to your Savior or to your Judge. The Lord Jesus himself warned us about it. He longs for us to be ready, and says: "Be always on the watch, and pray that you may be able to escape all that is about to happen, and that you may be able to stand before the Son of Man" (Luke 21:36).

The clearest sign is that the Jews have returned to their own country. I was in California on the morning that the state of Israel was born (or reborn) on May 15, 1948. My host read it in the morning paper and she ran to the phone. She called her friends and said, "Have you read the paper? The state of Israel has been established. Jesus will come very soon; let's make sure we are ready and that as many others as possible are ready too." That woman saw the event, as it were, from God's perspective, from the perspective of the Bible.

Here are just a few other signs of the times. "Many will go here and there to increase knowledge" (Dan. 12:4). What incredible knowledge we have nowadays. Even if there is a quake on the moon, we know about it here on earth because of the seismograph that we left on the moon. Another sign is that the pure will become purer and the vile become more vile (see

Revelation 22:11). Everything is heading toward a climax. I have never before met such dedicated young Christians as now, who are prepared to live for Jesus and to die if necessary. But I have also never seen, read, or heard so much filth and impurity as now.

But that is enough about the signs of the times. Now we'll see how you can be ready. In Philippians 1:9–11 it says, "And this is my prayer: that your love may abound more and more in knowledge and depth of insight, so that you may be able to discern what is best and may be pure and blameless until the day of Christ, filled with the fruit of righteousness that comes through Jesus Christ—to the glory and praise of God."

Is that possible—such abundant love in your heart and mine? We can never manage it ourselves. No, you and I can't, but the Holy Spirit can. Read about it for yourself in Romans 5:1–11. From verse 5 onward it says, "And hope does not disappoint us, because God has poured out his love into our hearts by the Holy Spirit, whom he has given us. You see, at just the right time, when we were still powerless, Christ died for the ungodly.... Since we have now been justified by his blood, how much more shall we be saved from God's wrath through him!"

The Holy Spirit has been given to us. Does the Holy Spirit have you? Then you will be filled. He is prepared to fill you just as light fills a room when you open the curtains. Not a small corner, but all the doors, all the drawers must be open. The Lord Jesus wants to live in your heart and in your life through His Holy Spirit. You can't experience His victory at work, in the kitchen, or in the bedroom, if you only open the door of your living room.

Some people think that complete surrender is possible only for people who work full-time in evangelism, such as missionaries, preachers, and pastors. But everyone can and must be prepared for Jesus' second coming. My father had a watch-maker's shop. He sometimes said, "I am a watchmaker by the grace of God." I worked with him for twenty-five years in the business and I saw and experienced how a person who is first of all a Christian, and then a businessman, lives. Father longed for Jesus' return. All his prayers ended with these words: "And, Father, may the moment soon come when Jesus Christ, Your precious Son, returns on the clouds of heaven."

Yes, everyone can live in full surrender to the Lord; you too! John says, "And now, dear children, continue in him, so that when he appears we may be confident and unashamed before him at his coming" (1 John 2:28). Jesus is knocking on the door of your heart at this very moment. Will you say, "Yes, Lord Jesus, come into my heart"? Then He will come and He will do it. He longs for you, He loves you. He longs for us to be prepared for His return even more than we long for and prepare for it.

In John 15:5 He says, "If a man remains in me and I in him, he will bear much fruit; apart from me you can do nothing." You yourself can't prepare yourself for Jesus' return. But stop compromising. In your heart there is a cross and a throne. If the "self" is on the throne, then Jesus is on the cross. If Jesus is on the throne, then the "self" is on the cross; and He, Jesus, will "keep you strong to the end, so that you will be blameless on the day of our Lord Jesus Christ" (1 Cor. 1:8). Hallelujah, He will do it, He will overcome. He is going to make all things new. Jesus makes us more than conquerors at the new begin-ning, the coming of the kingdom of Peace on earth.

"Lord Jesus, thank You that You will answer the prayers of everyone who says, 'Yes, Lord Jesus, come into my heart, fill me with Your Spirit, prepare me for Your return. Take my life.' Hallelujah, what a wonderful Savior. Amen."

Twenty-Four

Joy in the Darkness

꒰

If it's dark everywhere, you can become so discouraged. You might doubt whether light still exists. But even if you can't see the Lord, He sees you and me. Jesus said, "And surely I am with you always, to the very end of the age" (Matt. 28:20). When it's necessary, He suddenly says, "I'm still here!"

I was in Vietnam, in an airport departure lounge. We had to arrive very early in the morning to book our seats on the military transport planes. The only way to travel in South Vietnam during the war was with soldiers in relatively primitive planes. I was sleepy and tired; it was so very early in the morning. It was sweltering and humid. I was sitting between soldiers in their slovenly uniforms. There was a constant deafening noise of engines as planes took off and landed. In the distance I heard shooting; from time to time you could hear bombs dropping. The radio was playing noisy music. On a notice board I read: "During enemy attacks go immediately to the air raid shelter in this corridor." Everything was so terribly sad; I could have cried.

It suddenly became quiet. All the planes had taken off. Then the music on the radio stopped and a calm voice began to read a morning devotional based on Psalm 51: "Let me hear joy and gladness; . . . create in me a pure heart, O God, and renew a steadfast spirit within me." It was just as if God was saying, "I'm still here!" I sat straight up and listened: "Restore to me the joy of your salvation . . . and sinners will turn back to you . . . a broken and contrite heart, O God, you will not despise." It was just like a very tiny piece of heaven in the middle of hell. I suddenly became very happy. I wasn't at all surprised when, at the end of the devotional, a song was sung to the tune of "Ode to Joy" from Beethoven's Ninth Symphony.

In the afternoon I was in Da Nang, close to the front line. I spoke to the soldiers and told them of the joy that passes all understanding and that you can have that joy in all circumstances, if you will only put your hand in Jesus' strong hand. He creates in you a clean heart and renews a steadfast spirit within you. A broken and contrite heart He does not despise. He says: "Come to me, all you who are weary and burdened, and I will give you rest" (Matt. 11:28). I told them of a very dark point in time on this earth, when Jesus said, "It is finished," and then died on a cross. He had suffered all that was necessary to save us from sin and guilt. That is why we can say: the joy of the Lord will be our strength, whatever may happen. Many soldiers laid their hand in the hand of Jesus, and when they left several of them said, "Till we meet again, maybe not here, but up in heaven." I don't know how many of them are already there.

Let us pray: "Thank You, Lord Jesus, that we know that You are here, today—for us, for the people in Vietnam, Israel, Egypt, yes, everywhere, to the ends of the earth. Thank You that You came into the world as a Light, so that whoever believes in You does not remain in darkness. Make us joyful about that, so that we can be lights in this dark world, wherever You call us to be. Hallelujah. Thank You, Lord Jesus. Amen."

Twenty-Five

Come and See Jesus

The next day Jesus decided to leave for Galilee. Finding Philip, he said to him, "Follow me." Philip, like Andrew and Peter, was from the town of Bethsaida. Philip found Nathanael and told him, "We have found the one Moses wrote about in the Law, and about whom the prophets also wrote—Jesus of Nazareth, the son of Joseph." "Nazareth! Can anything good come from there?" Nathanael asked. "Come and see," said Philip. When Jesus saw Nathanael approaching, he said of him, "Here is a true Israelite, in whom there is nothing false." "How do you know me?" Nathanael asked. Jesus answered, "I saw you while you were still under the fig tree before Philip called you." Then Nathanael declared, "Rabbi, you are the Son of God; you are the King of Israel." Jesus said, "You believe because I told you I saw you under the fig tree. You shall see greater things than that." He then added, "I tell you the truth, you shall see heaven open, and the angels of God ascending and descending on the Son of Man."

—JOHN 1:43–51

Come and see," said Philip.

Have you ever said that to somebody? Come and see Jesus. Wasn't that marvelous? I believe that the most wonderful thing that can happen to a child of God is to lead someone to Jesus. You then know for sure that you have not lived in vain.

I am so thankful for Acts 1 verse 8; there the Lord Jesus commissioned us to be His witnesses in Jerusalem, Judea, Samaria, and to the ends of the earth. It's no small thing, the task of worldwide evangelism!

But first of all the equipping: He gave us all that we need for the task; "You will receive power when the Holy Spirit comes on you" (Acts 1:8). The Holy Spirit, His power, supplies us with all we need to be disciples ourselves and to disciple others. We can't do it, but He can. That's why it is so very important that we are filled with the Holy Spirit. Full, right up to the very last corner of our lives. It is only possible if the very last corner of our lives is completely surrendered to the Lord Jesus.

If we allow Him to live only in our study or living room, then He can't help and protect us in our kitchen or bedroom. Yes, I know, He sometimes does protect us, even if we don't invite Him to do so. But we can only expect to be more than conquerors everywhere and to be mirrors of His love and joy, if we walk hand in hand with Him through the whole house of our lives from the basement to the attic. Then He not only helps support us, He carries us Himself.

Care is powerful. His strength shows through our weakness. I once spent two months in Vietnam and Indonesia. The boiling hot climate, difficult travel, and all the tragedies I saw (plus those I did not personally witness but heard about) made me ill and I felt my age. Sometimes I felt unable to go on. But there were blessings such as I have seldom experienced. It was the power of the Holy Spirit that did it and that was even more evident because I was unable to carry on in my own strength. I was able to share the great riches of the Gospel everywhere, with soldiers, forest dwellers, and missionaries. I saw that the Lord used me to bring comfort, encouragement, and to prepare people to face death. The people listened not to Corrie ten Boom but to the Lord Jesus who spoke through me by His Holy Spirit.

Would you like the Lord to speak through you today? If you don't know Him yet, then I say as Philip did: Come and see Jesus! He loves you and died for you on the cross. So bring your sins to Him and then let Him in by opening all the doors, from the basement to the attic.

"Lord Jesus, I thank You that You have never sent away a single sinner who came to You for forgiveness. Thank You that You have given us such a wonderful task of being disciples and making others disciples. Lord Jesus, hear the readers who now pray: 'Lord, work through me today with Your conquering love, so that we together, You and I, can invite others to come and see.' Thank You, Lord Jesus. Hallelujah. Amen."

Twenty-Six

A Glorious Future

༞

And this gospel of the kingdom will be preached in the whole world as a testimony to all nations, and then the end will come" (Matt. 24:14). When I read this text today, I suddenly realized that we can all work toward hastening Jesus' return.

Do you, too, long for that glorious future, in which the Lord Jesus will make all things new, as it says in Revelation 21:5? When this earth will be covered with the knowledge of the Lord as the waters cover the sea (see Habakkuk 2:14). Just imagine how wonderful it will be when we see Him face-to-face.

Everything is so distressing and uncertain in this world. I love to think of these promises; because it is going to happen, maybe very soon. There is so much comfort for those who are prepared. Read Revelation 21:3–5: "And I heard a loud voice from the throne saying, 'Now the dwelling of God is with men, and he will live with them. They will be his people, and God himself will be with them and be their God. He will wipe every tear from their eyes. There will be no more death or mourning or crying or pain, for the old order of things has passed away.' He who was seated on the throne said, 'I am making everything new!'"

These things are trustworthy and true, just as all the deeply serious incidents these days, in Israel and the countries around it, are truly happening. We are living in apocalyptic days; I mean days about which the last book of the Bible has much to say.

When Paul wrote about the gathering up of believers, he said, "Therefore encourage each other with these words" (1 Thess. 4:18). We need comfort and encouragement these days.

I once worked for a year with Dr. J. Edwin Orr. He is a small Irishman, who as a twenty-year-old travelled all over the world on his bicycle to spread the Gospel. He has worked in 140 countries. He once said, "I believe that God has not set a precise date for Jesus' return, but has established a plan in which a great number of people must hear the Gospel before He returns." If that is the case, and, from our text you can assume it is, then we have a great responsibility.

The person you meet today could be the last. But we should be prepared and willing to witness not just because of that. Every child of God has a task to fulfill: "Therefore go and make disciples of all nations" (Matt. 28:19). The Lord Jesus said this before His ascension. A disciple works on his Master's business. You in your small corner and I in mine. My corner happens to move all over the world; yours may be in your own home, office, or street.

But do our encounters with others produce fruit? A Christian who is never used to lead someone to Christ is unnatural. We have a wonderful task on this planet to be the light of the world and the salt of the earth. Tell someone today that the Lord Jesus carried the sins of the whole world on the cross—for him or for her too. Tell them that He said this with great love and warmth and that He meant it when He said, "Come to me, all you who are weary and burdened, and I will give you rest," and "whoever comes to me I will never drive away" (Matt. 11:28; John 6:37).

"Thank You, Lord Jesus, that You want to use us to show others the way to heaven. Thank You that if we have never found the way ourselves, You invite us to come today. We now pray together, Lord, for the people we will meet today. Will You please prepare their hearts for Your message? Prepare our hearts to be channels of living water. Shine on them, through us, with Your love. There is so much sadness and sorrow in the hearts and lives of most of the people we meet. Thank You that the fruit of the Spirit is love, joy, peace, patience, kindness, goodness, faithfulness, gentleness, and self-control—exactly what we and they need. Hallelujah, thank You, Lord. Amen."

Reflections
of
God's Glory

Corrie ten Boom at the microphone, broadcasting for Trans World Radio. (photo credit: Hans van der Steen, used by permission of Trans World Radio, Netherlands and Belgium)

Corrie ten Boom

Reflections of God's Glory

NEWLY DISCOVERED MEDITATIONS BY THE AUTHOR OF *THE HIDING PLACE*

ZondervanPublishingHouse
Grand Rapids, Michigan

A Division of HarperCollinsPublishers

Reflections of God's Glory
Copyright © 1999 by Stichting Trans World Radio voor Nederland en België

Requests for information should be addressed to:

📇 **Zondervan Publishing House**
Grand Rapids, Michigan 49530

Library of Congress Cataloging-in-Publication Data

Ten Boom, Corrie.
    Reflections of God's glory : newly discovered meditations / Corrie ten Boom.
        p.   cm.
    ISBN 0–310–22541–8 (alk. paper)
    1. Christian life—reformed authors. I. Title.
BV4501.2.T385 1999
242—dc21
                                                                98–31597
                                                                    CIP

Printed in the United States of America

99 00 01 02 03 04 05 /❖ DC/ 10 9 8 7 6 5 4 3 2 1

Contents

Acknowledgments

$\mathcal{S}$pecial thanks to:

Rinse Postuma, Director, Trans World Radio voor Nederland en België (Netherlands and Belgium), for special permission to translate and publish these manuscripts in English;

Clara M. van Dijk, Trans World Radio voor Nederland en België, for organizing, researching, and editing the original Dutch manuscripts;

Claire L. Rothrock, Trans World Radio-Europe, The Netherlands, for translation of all manuscripts from Dutch to English;

Hans van der Steen, Retired Director, Trans World Radio voor Nederland en België, for his valuable assistance to this project and for sharing many insights into the life and ministry of Corrie ten Boom gained from his personal relationship with Corrie formed through years of co-producing her radio broadcasts.

Tom Watkins, Trans World Radio-North America, for initiating and overseeing this project, and for editing the final manuscript.

γ

Introduction

$\mathcal{D}$inner was over and the clean up underway. Having guests for dinner was a very commonplace occurrence in the Lowell household on the island of Bonaire in the Caribbean. But on this night our four children quickly recognized that this was no ordinary visitor.

She insisted the kids call her "Tante" (Auntie) Corrie. After excusing herself to the living room, she sat in an old wooden rocker, opened a large purse, and pulled out a purple piece of cloth. Corrie ten Boom invited the children to sit at her feet and proceeded to talk about life—her life—and the challenges she and her family faced during World War II in her German-occupied town of Haarlem in the Netherlands.

As she spoke, she slowly unfolded the purple cloth in her hands and revealed hundreds of strings tied in knots pulled through the cloth. It all looked so random. She showed the children how the strings didn't seem to make sense from where they sat at her feet on the floor of the living room. "That's the whole point," she exclaimed. She said it was because of our limited vision, our limited perspective of what God is doing in our lives, that we question Him. At that point Tante Corrie slowly turned the purple tangled mess around to reveal a beautiful tapestry: a crown of gold with multi-colored jewels.

"This," she said, "is what God sees ... from His perspective ... a masterpiece!"

During a visit to Bonaire in 1973, Corrie ten Boom shared this now-famous illustration of God's sovereignty. She had begun broadcasting radio messages in her native Dutch language to the Netherlands over Trans World Radio in 1966. Now, broadcasts had also been added to the Dutch-speaking Antilles islands from our station on Bonaire, and she wanted to see the station first-hand.

Fast forward, for a moment, to a cool, overcast midsummer day in 1996—thirteen years after Corrie's death. One of our staff members from the United States was visiting Trans World Radio's office in Voorthuizen, the Netherlands, when another, quite dramatic, introduction took place. As this guest was handed a book of Corrie ten Boom's radio messages published in Dutch by TWR–Netherlands and saw a stack of Corrie's typewritten radio scripts in a corner of the office there, the realization hit that no English-speaking person had ever had the benefit of hearing or reading these messages penned by a true giant of the Christian faith.

Thus began the odyssey that led to the publishing of Reflections of God's Glory, a collection of twenty-four radio messages Corrie aired in Dutch over Trans World Radio beginning three decades ago, never before translated into English.

Yet, the story of Corrie ten Boom goes back much further than either Voorthuizen or Bonaire. It was on February 28, 1944, that the lives of the Ten Boom family of Haarlem changed forever. On that day, Corrie, her father, her older sister, and thirty-five other people were arrested and sent to a Nazi concentration camp for not disclosing the whereabouts of six Jews hidden in a secret room attached to her bedroom. Corrie, the daughter of a watchmaker, and her devoutly Christian family dedicated much of their efforts toward shielding Jews from Nazi persecution during the German occupation of the Netherlands in World War II. They were imprisoned and subjected to the atrocities of the Ravensbrück concentration camp in Germany, where Corrie's father and sister, Betsie, died. Corrie was inexplicably released after ten months of incarceration. She later found out that an order had been given at the end of the very week of her release to kill all women her age and older. God had used an error in prison paperwork as the catalyst to release her.

Corrie's unlikely voice arose from the ashes of post-World War II Europe, proclaiming the transforming message of God's love and forgiveness over the airwaves of Trans World Radio, an international Christian broadcasting ministry founded in the United States in 1952. She is most closely identified with her best-selling book The Hiding Place, which was later made into a full-length movie, and she gained worldwide acclaim as a Christian writer and speaker for her deep yet practical spiritual insights gleaned from her life experiences. At the time of her death in 1983, Corrie had written nine books, spoken in more than sixty countries, and produced five films.

Twenty-two years after her release from Ravensbrück, Corrie had the rare privilege of beginning a ministry of broadcasting the Good News of God's redeeming love via a powerful transmitting site in Monte Carlo utilized by Trans World Radio. Ironically, the Monte Carlo station was originally built by Adolph Hitler for his Nazi propaganda machine, but never used for his sinister purposes. Instead, God used it as an open door for Corrie to proclaim to millions worldwide her story of how God's grace sustained her during her deepest hours of despair and how He empowered her to forgive those responsible for the deaths of her father and sister.

Later, the broadcast followed from TWR–Bonaire as well as from TWR–Swaziland in Africa. Her messages were also copied onto cassettes and put into print. In addition to her popular radio talks, the text of The Hiding Place was broadcast over TWR–Monte Carlo and TWR–Bonaire.

Throughout the years since the initial broadcast in 1954 from Tangier, Morocco, and its first program from Monte Carlo in 1960, TWR has been blessed with missions-minded broadcasters such as Corrie ten Boom. Today, more than 250 cooperating broadcasters worldwide air their programs via TWR.

Utilizing forty transmitters from twelve primary sites and by satellite to three continents, TWR broadcasts more than 1,200 hours of gospel programs each week in over 140 languages. Each year more than 1.4 million letters are received from listeners in over 160 countries.

Radio is personal and private. It overcomes geographical, political, religious, social, and educational barriers—oftentimes in places inaccessible to missionaries or where open evangelism is risky, restricted, or banned. It also speaks the language of the intended audience. As a result, missionary radio is one the most cost-effective ways to reach people for Jesus Christ.

To discover more about the global life-changing ministry of Trans World Radio, you can write to TWR at P.O. Box 8700, Cary, NC 27512, or P.O. Box 310, London, Ontario, N6A 4W1. Or you can email us at info@twr.org. You can also learn more through the Internet at www.twr.org.

It is a singular privilege that Trans World Radio has been given, sixteen years after Corrie's death, to have a part in bringing to readers in the United States and around the world what are, in effect, fresh, new insights from the pen of Corrie ten Boom. The timeless meditations in this book are the same rich, practical applications into living the Christian life that a generation of those familiar with Corrie's ministry have come to love and expect. It is our desire that a new generation of readers will come to love and appreciate with equal fervor the unique and insightful qualities of the writings of Corrie ten Boom.

THOMAS J. LOWELL, PRESIDENT, TRANS WORLD RADIO

CARY, NORTH CAROLINA

NOVEMBER 1998

Foreword

We were in the middle of a Trans World Radio-Netherlands board meeting, being of course carried on in the Dutch language. Suddenly I heard a voice say in English, "Lord, this is really a big problem we have here." It was Corrie ten Boom who was seated next to me, and who quite naturally switched from talking to the board in Dutch to talking to the Lord in English. This was so typically Corrie. She had that refreshingly unique, practical, simple, spiritual walk with her Lord that allowed her to move in a carefree way from grappling with a problem to involving her Lord in a solution.

The story of Corrie ten Boom and Trans World Radio actually started in 1965 at a Trans World Radio triennial conference in Monte Carlo attended by our Dutch director, Hans van der Steen. Music at that conference was supplied by the Peter van Woerden family. On one of the days of the conference, Peter came to Hans and handed him some messages from his Aunt Corrie ten Boom, suggesting that perhaps he would want to use them over the air in the Trans World Radio Dutch programs.

Upon his return to Holland, Hans contacted Corrie to request permission to use the material. Corrie's response was, "Why don't you come and let's talk?" When they got together, one of the first questions Corrie asked Hans was, "How did you join TWR?"

The story of Hans and Janny van der Steen's leaving the Phillips Company, and by faith joining Trans World Radio to establish our partner organization in The Netherlands, is an unbelievable testimony of God's miraculous provision. For example, the studio equipment for the first TWR-Netherlands recording studio came from the Phillips Company as they sent Hans on his way to his new life calling.

Once, even a new car was delivered to their door by an anonymous donor!

In the midst of Hans telling this story to Corrie, she said, "Just stop right there." She then called her personal assistant who was upstairs at the time, saying, "Come down and listen to the foolishness of God!" This started a unique relationship between Trans World Radio and Corrie ten Boom, which began with the airing of the first of Corrie's messages on May 14, 1966.

Hans would go to Corrie's home to record the messages. Corrie's involvement in broadcasting over TWR expanded to our station on Bonaire after a visit by Corrie to the Caribbean island, which led to the placing of a burden on her heart to reach the many Dutch-speaking people in The Netherlands Antilles and Suriname. One of her message series was the reading over the air of *The Hiding Place*, the book describing so compellingly her God-blessed life.

Listeners loved her messages. In fact, Hans readily admits to the fact that most of the mail response to the Dutch programs was from Corrie's contributions. Her style was practical and basic, enabling everyone to understand. Corrie's special gift was the ability to include personal illustrations that so clearly depicted the points she was making. Years later, Corrie would still tell of the people she met in her travels who had been so blessed by those "early days" radio programs.

Hans remembered in particular a time when Corrie decided to do a series about the devil. She was to title the messages, "Tricks of the Devil." This decision triggered a series of circumstances which could only be described as an attempt by Satan to avoid the production of these programs. It all started with a serious car accident involving Corrie, just one day before the programs were to be recorded. This ultimately postponed the series for four months. Finally when the recording was underway Hans commented, "Every time we started recording, there would be a banging noise as if someone was working on the central heating system." In fact, this was not the case. However, the interference was so persistent throughout the day that it took an entire afternoon to record only four eight-minute messages. Clearly Corrie had something to say that Satan did not want her to share.

I believe as you read this unique series of Corrie ten Boom's messages, you will quickly recognize the special gift that she brought to the Kingdom, of presenting practical lessons for daily living.

WILLIAM P. MIAL, ASSISTANT TO THE PRESIDENT
FORMER DIRECTOR OF TRANS WORLD RADIO-EUROPE
CARY, NORTH CAROLINA
APRIL 1998

One

A Mirror of God's Glory

And we, who with unveiled faces all reflect the Lord's glory, are being transformed into his likeness with ever-increasing glory, which comes from the Lord, who is the Spirit.

—*2 Corinthians 3:18*

Have you ever seen a portrait of Sadhu Sundar Singh? That man had such a holy face that I can imagine the Lord Jesus looked like that. He spent much time alone with the Lord in prayer, in meditation, and in fasting. He had visions that give us a picture of heaven. Sadhu Sundar Singh lived according to the Bible. Yes, he was a mirror of the glory of the Lord.

But now I want to speak of you and me, because verse 18 says "we," and that includes you and me. One day we will all share in the nature of the glorified body of Jesus. I can imagine that one of you might say, "Look, I am so worried! Sadhu, yes . . . , but I am so busy. I have six children and no time to be quiet. I can't say that I'm a mirror of the Lord Jesus. I don't look at Him enough." Someone else might say, "I have a very strong ego; I insist on my rights and am easily offended. I feel slighted when people don't greet me. I can't see how I can become like Jesus."

I know, the Bible says, " . . . our citizenship is in heaven. And we eagerly await a Savior from there, the Lord Jesus Christ, who, by the power that enables him to bring everything under his control, will transform our lowly bodies so that they will be like his glorious body" (Phil. 3:20–21). Despite this promise, I understand that someone might confess, "I have a jealous nature. I hide it as much as possible, but I am afraid that it can sometimes be read all over my face. I am afraid that I don't reflect the glory of the Lord." Others might admit, "I like to smoke cigarettes or drink, all very respectably, but I am addicted to it. I don't really feel like a citizen of heaven," or "I like to look good. I think it's wonderful if people appreciate me and think well of me. Being transformed with ever increasing glory would be fine, but taking up that despised cross behind Jesus . . . no, I can't have too much of that."

Well, fill in your confession. You may feel that your character, your circumstances, your experiences are anything but a growing process of being transformed into the likeness of Jesus, continually becoming more and more a mirror of the glory of the Lord. Should we just leave it up to others? To a Sadhu, or to people we know who are further down the road toward sanctification—people who are permanently filled with the Holy Spirit and are such wide-open channels of streams of living water. Yes, if it was up to you and me, I'd agree, "Yes. Let's be level-headed and keep our feet on the ground."

But it doesn't just depend on you and me! I am going to get the answer from the Bible. Read it yourself, then you'll see that it isn't Corrie ten Boom's answer but God's. Philippians 3:20–21 tells us about someone who has the power that enables Him to bring everything under His control.

I once talked to Dr. Elly Beerman-de Roos, an experienced counselor, about a problem that seemed insurmountable to me. "Nothing will come of it," I said. Then she struck her fist on the table and said, "What? He who rose from the dead and rolled away a heavy stone from the grave does not have the power to deal with your problem?" I was ashamed of myself and saw the reality of Jesus' victory. The power which enables Him to bring everything under His control is strong enough for Him to take you and me, who are so busy with our work, by the hand and lead us into silence. " . . . He who began a good work in you will carry it on to completion until the day of Christ Jesus" (Phil.1:6).

We with our worries, you with your strong ego, and you with your jealous nature, the power that enables Him to bring everything under His control can conquer our sins. Jesus loves sinners! You with your cigarette that is slowly causing lung cancer; you with your drink that makes you a danger when you drive a car; you with your vanity—there is someone who will "keep you strong to the end, so that you will be blameless on the day of our Lord Jesus Christ" (1 Cor. 1:8).

He can do it! What do we have to do? Place our weak hand in His strong hand. Open all the corners, drawers, and rooms of our life for Him so that His victory is not just experienced in one room or in a particular circumstance. No, open all the windows to the light. Don't leave one corner in the dark. Open everything to Him! In 2 Timothy 1:12 we read, " . . . I know whom I have believed, and am convinced that he is able to guard what I have entrusted to him for that day."

Give yourself again or for the first time, but this time completely, to Him of whom it is said in 1 Thessalonians 5:23–24, "May God himself, the God of peace, sanctify you through and through. May your whole spirit, soul and body be kept blameless at the coming of our Lord Jesus Christ. The one who calls you is faithful and he will do it." He will do it through the power that enables Him to bring everything under His control. That counts for us, you and me; for all of us, no exceptions!

"Thank You, Lord Jesus, that Your power is so great that I can do all things through You who gives me strength. Amen."

Two

The Lord's Garden

In the basement of a large tenement house in which many families lived, there was an old broken harp. People had often tried to repair it and play it, but no one had ever succeeded in doing so. One day a beggar came and asked for shelter. The only place for him to spend the night was in a corner of that basement. Late that night people heard the sound of beautiful music coming from the basement. They found the beggar there playing the harp, and they asked, "How were you able to repair the harp and play it so beautifully?" He replied, "I made this harp myself. When I was young, I made lots of harps. This is one of my harps. Shouldn't I be able to repair something I made myself?" John 1:10 says that Jesus "was in the world, and . . . the world was made through him." We have been created by His hands. I despair when I try to change myself and patch myself up. I can't do it and never will be able to do it, but if I surrender myself to Him who made me, I experience miracles!

Charles Spurgeon once said, "What a privilege it is to know that I am a field under heavenly cultivation—not a wilderness but a garden of the Lord, walled by grace, planted according to a divine plan, worked by love, weeded by heavenly discipline, and constantly protected by divine power. A soul, so privileged, is prepared to bring forth fruit to the glory of God." Yes, as Paul says, "You are God's field, God's building" (1 Cor. 3:9). You are a field under heavenly cultivation, walled by grace. We see that grace when we look at the cross of Golgotha. There God's Son bore the sins of the whole world, your sins and mine. But we also see that grace when we look at the empty grave. We have a living Savior, who is with us, who looks at us and loves us, who forgives us if we confess our sins and cleanses us with His blood— what grace! Ephesians 1:7 says of Jesus, "In him we have redemption through his blood, the forgiveness of sins, in accordance with the riches of God's grace. . . ."

We have been planted according to a divine pattern, even if we do not always understand that pattern. God is interested in each of us "microscopically" as well as "telescopically." The hairs of our heads have been counted, but the universe is also in His hand.

Yes, our life is like a garden of the Lord, walled by grace, cultivated by love, and weeded by heavenly discipline. Sin comes between us and God, like the weeds that impede the growth of plants and flowers. Heavenly discipline cultivates us by pulling out the weeds. These can be difficult times in one's life.

I was in a jail cell all alone for four months. That was a time of plowing. I thought, "There'll be nothing left of me." I was desperate, but I suddenly saw God's side of things. I saw myself as a field that was being plowed and weeded. I wrote about this experience in a letter:

"Amazingly I have adapted to this lonely life, together with God. I often speak to my Savior and am gaining more insight into time and eternity. I am prepared to be with Christ in life and in death—that is the best! But life here with Him attracts me too; and I am longing for action. Oh, that continual communion with the Savior—I am thankful that I am alone; me who loves company. I see my sins more clearly, for example my own Ego (with a capital E) and much superficiality.

I once begged for deliverance, but the Lord said, "My grace is sufficient for you." I continue to look to Him and try not to be impatient. I won't be here a moment longer than God thinks is necessary. Pray for me that I will be able to wait for His timing. Life here has wonderful proportions; time is here only to be lived through. It amazes me that I have adapted so well. Some things I can never get used to, but in general I am very happy. It is dark, but then the Savior gives His light and that is wonderful."

My brother was in the same jail during the war and knew what could happen to prisoners there. He came out of jail a sick man and died of that illness a year later. He had the ability to see things from God's perspective, that he was a field under heavenly cultivation. During this time, in which he felt the plowshare and weeding, he wrote in a song that even such hard times can be wonderful because Christ, the Lord, is fighting for His people.

In jail we prisoners lived close to death. When I was in a Nazi concentration camp, I lived for four months in the shadow of a crematorium. There was something liberating about that. You see things in the right proportion because you touch eternity; and then you see everything in the light of eternity. Weeding can hurt. It can wound you, but we are victorious through the blood of the Lamb. We are like clay in the hands of the Potter who shapes, molds, and models us. Don't forget, we are being cultivated and weeded, but our field is constantly under the safe protection of God's omnipotence and His caring love!

The Dutch poet, Bilderdijk once said, "God cares for us with the most exceptional providence."

A soul so prepared is ready to bring forth fruit to the glory of God. What are you? A wilderness or a garden for the Lord? If you are a wilderness, come to Jesus; He will not reject you. He has changed many wildernesses into gardens full of flowers and fruit.

He can make you into a garden under heavenly cultivation, walled by grace, planted according to a divine pattern, tilled by love, weeded by heavenly discipline, and protected by divine omnipotence.

We pray, "Thank You, Lord, that all 'wilderness' people can come to You, and that You don't reject them. You cultivate them to make them into a garden of the Lord, with much fruit and beautiful flowers, by Your Holy Spirit. And the fruit of the Spirit is love, joy, peace, kindness, patience, goodness, faithfulness, gentleness, and self-control. And Lord, then You can use them wonderfully in this 'wilderness' world to feed and empower others. Listen, Lord, to each one who now prays, 'Lord Jesus, my life looks more like a wilderness than a garden. Fill me with Your Holy Spirit so that from now on I can receive power to be a faithful, cheerful witness who bears fruit.' Thank You that in Your Word You say that whoever prays for the Holy Spirit can be sure of receiving Him. Hallelujah! Amen."

Three

Can You Forgive?

Matthew 6:14–15 says, "For if you forgive men when they sin against you, your heavenly Father will also forgive you. But if you do not forgive men their sins, your Father will not forgive your sins."

Can you forgive? I can't, but Jesus in me, and Jesus in you, can! Some time ago in America I talked about a great miracle I experienced. When Jesus tells you to love your enemies, He himself gives you that love. I told of how I met a very cruel man in Germany who made my sister suffer a lot when she was dying in a German concentration camp. This man told me the wonderful news that he had found Jesus and had brought all his awful sins to Him. "I know," he said, "that in the Bible it says that Jesus died for the sins of the whole world, for my sins too. When I read 1 John 1:7–9—'The blood of Jesus, his [God's] Son, purifies us from all sin . . . If we confess our sins, he is faithful and just and will forgive us our sins and purify us from all unrighteousness'—I, who had been so terribly cruel, dared to do it. I confessed all my sins and believed that Jesus would purify even my heart by His blood. Then I asked if He would give me the grace to ask one of my victims, who had suffered through my cruelties, for forgiveness."

Then the man asked me, "Fraülein ten Boom, will you forgive me for my cruelties?" I could not do so. It made me bitter to think of what he had done and how my sister Betsie had suffered. Then I prayed, "Lord Jesus, thank You for Romans 5:5 [about how God has poured out His love into our hearts by the Holy Spirit]; thank You that God's love takes away my bitterness." Then a miracle happened. It was as if I felt God's love flowing through my arm. I was able to forgive that man and even shake his hand. You never experience God's love more marvelously than at the moment He gives you love for your enemies.

In America, a lady approached me after I had spoken about this text. She handed me a key. "Will you please destroy this?" she asked. "Yes, but why?" She said, "It's the key to the home of a lady who stole the love of my husband." I do not know what her plans were—maybe to burst in on him and that woman, maybe to catch them red-handed, perhaps to take revenge. I know what happened when she gave me that key. She had forgiven them, and the Lord Jesus had performed the miracle of replacing hatred in her heart with God's love.

Recently, I have met many young people. Many of them had dreadful pasts—addiction to drugs, crime. I sometimes asked them, "Have you asked your parents to forgive you for the pain that you caused them in the past?" I also found that they themselves had to forgive. "Have you forgiven your parents for the bad things they did in your life?" I saw great deliverance when, in God's power, they straightened out problems between them and their parents and put away their bitterness and lack of forgiveness. It was wonderful to see how many young people were able to forgive and ask for forgiveness by the power of the Holy Spirit.

Such a shadow in our lives can keep us in bondage and make us so unhappy. Jesus came like a light in the darkness so that everyone who believes in Him will not remain in darkness. Is there the darkness of bitterness or guilt in your life? I would like to give you some advice: Straighten things out today! Ask for forgiveness and tell those who have hurt you that you have forgiven them too. Do it together with Jesus. He will do it. He is the Victor, and He makes you and me conquerors. The Lord Jesus will cause you to be a great blessing to those with whom you have not been able to get along.

Not only young people who do not know the Lord need this truth. Those of you who have known the Lord for a long time and have unforgiveness in your hearts: Come to Him and pray with me:

"Lord, will You show me if there is anything between You and me, between me and someone else, me and my parents, me and my children? Will You help me when I ask them for forgiveness and when I forgive them? Thank You for Your strong love because You said in Romans 5:5, 'God has poured out his love into our hearts by the Holy Spirit, whom he has given us.' Lord, I give everything to You—my past, my present, my future, my bitterness, everything. Thank You that You in me are the Victor! Amen."

Four

God's Answer to Worry

Today I am going to talk about worry and anxiety. My message is for Christians, but even if you are not a Christian, still listen because you will hear something of the richness that you inherit when you become a Christian! The path is open. Don't you realize that yet? He died on the cross for the sins of the whole world, for your sins. You can do it now—come to Jesus. The Bible says that whoever comes to Him will never be turned away. Believe in Him, and He will make you a child of God. That is the way to become a Christian.

When you become a Christian, the Lord will train you with great love. You see, being a Christian does not mean that you won't need to fight any battles. You are now a strategic target for the enemy. One of the most successful weapons of the devil is worry. To be a conqueror in that battle, you have to learn to listen to what the Bible says about fighting the enemy. I will talk about that and also share my experiences and those of other Christians. God speaks through His Word, but also through His children.

I once read that the lifestyle of a Christian should be one of victory, joy, and abundance. From our side, we require only a dose of need and openness to accept help from the Lord. The doors of heaven are open; so if I hold on to feelings that prevent me from living under an open heaven, then it is no wonder I feel depressed. I read these words when I was extremely miserable, and I was ashamed. I picked up my Bible and read Philippians 4:6–7: "Do not be anxious about anything, but in everything, by prayer and petition, with thanksgiving, present your requests to God. And the peace of God, which transcends all understanding, will guard your hearts and your minds in Christ Jesus." Suddenly I saw what the Lord meant. As children of the light, we have to live as people who are powerful, content, calm, and free. That is the task. The Bible says that the joy of the Lord will be our strength.

There is something else very practical: We have to take good note of the blessings He gives and has given. We can learn to count our blessings. The Bible says, "Do not be anxious about anything, but in everything, by prayer and petition, with thanksgiving, present your requests to God" (Phil. 4:6). Yes, that means prayer. Have you ever been discouraged about prayer? Worry is very frequently being concerned for others, and often, it can take a long time before you notice any response to prayer for others.

Some time ago, I had a wonderful experience. In a television broadcast with Willem Duys, a Dutch TV personality, I had a wonderful opportunity to share the Gospel with Dutch people. It was on Easter Sunday, in the evening. I was told that I may have given my Easter message to as many as six million people. Many people responded. I received phone calls, letters, and visits, and was able to do a lot of wonderful pastoral work. I was very encouraged.

I have experienced answers to prayer for more than seventy years. When I was five years old, I asked the Lord Jesus to come into my heart. He did so, and He has never forsaken me. I immediately became very concerned for people. Behind the Barteljorisstraat, where I lived, was the Smedestraat, where there were many bars. I saw many drunk people on the streets who were taken to the police station in the Smedestraat. I decided to do something about what I saw. I began to end every prayer with these words: "And Lord Jesus, will You save and convert the people in the Smedestraat?" After the television program, I received a letter from a woman who wrote, "My husband was so happy to hear that you were born in Haarlem. He lived in the Smedestraat for seventeen years and worked at the police station. He and I know the Lord Jesus too." An answer after seventy-three years.

I always went to Christian schools, but when I was fifteen years old, I went to a non-Christian school. I was there with pupils and teachers who did not know the Lord. How I talked to them, and moreover . . . how I prayed for them. Recently, I received a letter: "Do you know, Corrie, that sixty years ago we were at school together? I saw you on TV. I'd like to tell you that I am a follower of Jesus too." An answer after sixty years.

Another man phoned me: "Do you know that forty-five years ago you said the same thing to me as you said on TV? I always refused to do what you advised: Accept Jesus as my Savior. Now I believe I have to say 'yes' to Him. May I come and see you?" I replied, "Come quickly!" I prayed with him and said, "Ask the Lord Jesus to come into your heart." And he prayed, "Jesus, I can't get my heart open. Will you break the door down?" Jesus began a miracle in his life—an answer after forty-five years.

I also received a letter from a man who wrote these words: "Twenty-five years ago I came out of a concentration camp into the house that you had opened for ex-prisoners. You presented the Gospel to me, but I was not ready for it. I saw you on television, and I can now write to tell you that I have found the Lord"—an answer after twenty-five years.

Why am I telling you all this? So that you see how God's work is sometimes slow, but very sure. Don't be discouraged in your intercession for your son, husband, wife, daughter, or your neighbor, friend, or whoever you are concerned about. The devil will say to you, "Stop—you can surely see that God is not answering you." But the devil is a liar. Keep it up! I believe that when we get to heaven, we will see that not one prayer of intercession was lost. I have shared with you something of the joy of heaven in all those answers after so many years. Yes, the Bible says, "Cast your bread upon the waters, for after many days you will find it again" (Eccl. 11:1).

Shall we pray? "Thank You, Lord, that we can and must make our needs known to You through prayer and thanksgiving. You always listen, hear, and answer in Your time. Will You, by Your Holy Spirit, fill our hearts with faith instead of doubt? Thank You, Lord. Amen."

᠊ᢞ᠊

Five

Worrying Is Disobedient

Worrying is stupid. The Bible says, "Do not worry about anything." If you are worrying, you are being disobedient. I had to understand that before I could stop doing it. First, I tried in my own strength—positive thinking, not fretting anymore. That approach was about as successful as attacking a lion with a toy pistol! Only the Lord can set you free through the Holy Spirit. Ask for forgiveness. Be cleansed by the blood of the Lord Jesus and be filled by the Spirit, of whom Paul says, "God did not give us a spirit of timidity, but a spirit of power, of love and of self-discipline" (2 Tim. 1:7).

If the Bible is true—and it is true!—fear, worrying, and anxiety actually question the trustworthiness of God. Then apparently we are saying, "God, you are not speaking the truth." In other words, "You are lying." Will we believe what the Lord tells us in Philippians 4:19—"My God will meet all your needs according to his glorious riches in Christ Jesus"—and in Hebrews 13:5—". . . never will I leave you; never will I forsake you?" These promises allow us to say with confidence, "The Lord is my helper, I will not fear; what can man do to me?"

First Peter 5:7 says, "Cast all your anxiety on him because he cares for you," and Matthew 6:31–34 says, "So do not worry, saying, 'What shall we eat?' or 'What shall we drink?' or 'What shall we wear?' For the pagans run after all these things, and your heavenly Father knows that you need them. But seek first his kingdom and his righteousness, and all these things will be given to you as well. Therefore do not worry about tomorrow, for tomorrow will worry about itself. Each day has enough trouble of its own."

It was liberating when I understood that fear and worry are sin. No book in the world has such a wonderful answer to our problem of sin as does the Bible: Confess, let yourself be cleansed, and allow the Holy Spirit to control your heart, because the fruit of the Spirit is precisely the opposite of our sin. Galatians 5:22 says that the fruit of the Spirit is "love, joy, peace, patience, kindness, goodness, faithfulness, gentleness, and self-control."

The Lord Jesus gives a clear comparison in John 15. We are the branches, Jesus is the vine. Abiding—remaining—in Him is the secret. Jesus does the work of bearing fruit—Jesus, who bore our sins on the cross; Jesus, who is alive and whose Spirit lives in us; Jesus, the conqueror who makes us more than conquerors. I am weak; the devil is strong, but Jesus is much stronger than the devil. Therefore, Jesus and I together are much stronger than the devil, much stronger than the demon of worry.

Once, I had a burden that weighed heavily on me. I set it down and looked at it. Then I saw that everything about my burden was borrowed. One part belonged to the following day, one part to the next week. My burden was a huge, stupid mistake. I realized that worrying is carrying tomorrow's burden

with today's strength. It's carrying two days at once. It's pre-
maturely thinking of tomorrow. On the calendar, there is only
one day for action, and that is today.

Making plans is time-consuming. Time is necessary for making wise plans, but carrying them out belongs to only one day—
today. We become concerned about the future—our financial
concerns, our health. Where does this lead to? Nowhere.
Nowhere that is worth the trouble because tension ruins things.
It depletes the energy that you need to live today. The Holy
Spirit does not give you a clear blueprint for your life, but He
leads you from moment to moment. Live for today! The sun will
shine tomorrow on the problems that tomorrow brings.

I read somewhere, "Why don't we look for something that
is easier than anxiety? Worried people are like tightrope walk-
ers, trying to walk over a rope from the past to the future, bal-
ancing between hope and fear. In one hand they hold a bag
with the disordered past, in the other a bag, the feared future.
Worrying does not take away tomorrow's grief; it takes away
today's strength. It does not enable us to avoid evil, but it makes
us incapable of dealing with it when it comes."

I once heard a nice story, a kind of legend. A small clock,
which had just been finished by its maker, was put on a shelf in
his shop between two old clocks that were busily and loudly
ticking away the seconds. "So," said one of the old clocks to the
newcomer, "you've just started this task. I feel sorry for you. You
are bravely ticking now, but you'll be very tired once you've
ticked thirty-three million times."

"Thirty-three million ticks?" said the startled clock, "but I
could never do that!" He immediately stopped in desperation.

"Come on, stupid," said the other clock. "Why do you listen to such talk? That's not how things are. At each moment

you only need to tick once. Isn't that easy? And then again. That's just as easy. Carry on like that."

"Oh, if that's all," the new clock cried, "then that's easy enough. Off I go." And he began again to bravely tick each moment, without paying attention to the months and the millions of ticks. When the year was up, he had ticked thirty-three million times without realizing it.

Yes, living for the moment, that's what you need. The Lord's prayer says, "Give us today our daily bread." Deuteronomy 33:25 says, " . . . your strength will equal your days." That is a promise made more than three thousand years ago. A person does not fall so much because of the troubles of one day, but if tomorrow's burden is added, this load can become very, very heavy. It is wonderfully easy to live just for the day.

Shall we pray? "Lord Jesus, please teach us by Your Holy Spirit in us to live for today. Thank You that You forgive us if we ask forgiveness for the sin of worry, and that You set us free. Thank You that we know You are the Victor. Amen."

Six

The Miracle of Prayer
Is the Answer to Our Anxiety

If you accept the Lord Jesus, you are a child of God. Immediately, however, you also enter a battle, because the devil wants to entice you away from victorious life with Jesus. He tries to frighten you. But, fortunately, the Lord Jesus wants to fill your heart with His Holy Spirit, who gives us God's love (Rom. 5:5). Yes, God's love is poured out in our hearts by the Holy Spirit, and this love conquers fear and worry. When the Lord says in Isaiah 41:10, "Do not fear," He gives us the reason why that is possible. He says, "So do not fear, for I am with you; do not be dismayed, for I am your God. I will strengthen you and help you; I will uphold you with my righteous right hand." Are you sure that you are God's child? No? Then you must speak to the Lord Jesus today and ask Him into your heart, because then He will make you a child of God.

I want to speak again about worry and anxiety, and what that means to you if you are a child of God. Listen to what the Lord Jesus says in the Sermon on the Mount: "Therefore do not worry about tomorrow, for tomorrow will worry about itself. Each day has enough trouble of its own" (Matt. 6:34).

If you accept the Lord Jesus and follow Him, He will do a miracle in your life: the miracle of being born again. That means that to those who accept Jesus, He gives the right to become children of God. We are born into God's family, and we grow like children. One of the experiences of growth is that you accept the promises in the Bible and you obey the commandments that are so clearly stated in it. One of those commandments that gives such comfort is Matthew 6:34: " . . . do not worry about tomorrow." Through faith you have become a child of God, you have been saved, and through faith you also achieve victory over worry, fear, and other sins. Cast your burdens on the Lord. You do that when you pray.

Yes, prayer is so important. If possible, look for a place where you can be alone with the Lord and tell Him what you need. Pour your heart out to Him. Fine language is not necessary. If you are suffering from a nervous stomach, don't just ask the Lord to take away the stomach complaint, but tell Him what makes you nervous and pray about that. Pray specifically and expect a specific answer. If you ask God for bread, He will not give you a stone. If God does not answer right away, then go to Him again. Be thankful that you have a reason to go to Him again. Study the prayers in the Bible. They are not formal. They are spoken in ordinary language. Approach God as you would your mother, your father, a friend. Tell Him about your concerns; tell Him that you have sinned by worrying. Tell Him that you want victory over your anxiety. Make a clear choice. Believe in the Lord. It is not your prayer, but your Savior, who is the answer!

If you do not pray specifically, you trust more in the prayer than in the Lord. At least, it can be that way. Prayer is a family business, a child speaking to His Father. Prayer opens the door to Him who can and will save you from your worries. God's power is shown in our weakness. Galatians 1:16 says that Paul did not consult flesh and blood. Consulting people about your fears and worries—instead of bringing them to the Lord in prayer—can make them even bigger and heavier. Prayer is not meant to be one-way traffic. Imagine that someone comes in and asks you a question but then immediately turns around and leaves without waiting for an answer! We have to take time to speak with the Lord and to listen to His answer. We have to practice God's hidden companionship. Paul says in 2 Corinthians 10:5 that we have to take captive every thought to make it obedient to Christ. We have to do that, too, with our worries.

As well as prayer—the companionship of the Lord in your quiet time—there is another wonderful experience we can have: praying together. Praying together is extremely important. The Lord says that where two or three are gathered together in His name, there He is in the midst of them. The devil tries to hinder praying together in all kinds of ways.

I know of a small group of boys and girls in America who met together in the mornings to pray. They had seen lots of things go wrong at school. They soon noticed that the atmosphere in their class improved greatly after they had prayed. More and more young Christians joined them. After a time, they were forbidden to use the room. They looked for a quiet place where they could pray and found a cemetery near the school.

Winter came. They were very cold at the cemetery, but they carried on. One day the principal saw the students coming from the cemetery, and he asked them what they were doing there. They said that the cemetery was the only quiet place they could find where they could pray undisturbed. The principal was so touched that he opened a pleasant room for them where they could hold their prayer meeting each day. And that continues regularly. Miracles happen in that school. Instead of constant arguments between teachers and pupils, there is an atmosphere of unity. The principal told me this and said that he was sure this was the answer to the boys' and girls' prayers.

Shall we pray together? "Lord Jesus, how wonderful that You are a friend who understands our problems, and that we can tell You everything. Give us the opportunity to seek You and to find You by praying with others. Thank You that You gave us the promise: where two or three are gathered together in Your name, You are in the midst of them. Thank You. Amen."

Seven

Does God Answer Prayer?

Today I am speaking again to God's children. It is so wonderful to be a child of God. Listener, are you still not a child of God? Come to Jesus. He gives us the right to become a child of God. He did everything necessary for us to call God "Father." He did that when He carried our punishment on the Cross. Jesus is alive. He is with you. Speak to Him; He can hear you. Place your hand in His, and then He will make you a child of the King—God's child.

I want to talk to God's children about answered prayer. Years ago I spoke in Japan about the answer to our problem of worrying. I asked this question: "Do you know the feeling of worrying—feeling as if your heart was like a suitcase, heavy with your burdens?" I lifted up my suitcase and let them see how full it was with heavy objects. I told them that my heart felt like that last week. I read to them this glorious text: "Cast all your anxiety on him because he cares for you" (1 Peter 5:7). Then I took two objects out of the suitcase and laid them on the table. I said, "Here is the trip I am taking next week to a town where I don't know anyone. Will You give me strength and guidance? Will You lead me to Christians in that town who can show me the way around?" I took another object from my suitcase and laid it on the table, and I continued, "These are my friends at home. They wrote to me and told me that they had been in a car accident. Will You heal those who were injured? Here is the boy who refused to give his heart to You yesterday. Will You touch his heart?" As I named each concern, I took an object out of my case. After I unpacked everything, I said, "Amen." That's prayer. That's good.

But what I did after my "Amen" was not good! I packed all the objects on the table back into my suitcase. I explained that that's exactly what we do if we take our concerns to the Lord and then let those worries enter our hearts again. We must bring our burdens to Jesus and leave them there!

Fourteen years later, at an evangelistic conference, I met a Japanese man. He said, "Corrie ten Boom, when I see you, I think of your suitcase full of worries. I saw you that day when you unpacked your suitcase and then repacked the objects back into your suitcase. That experience taught me how to pray." A visible illustration stays in the memory for a long time.

Now I ask you: Have you unpacked your case of worries in your morning prayers? Good—your heavenly Father knows what you need. He who cares for a sparrow also cares for you (Matt. 10:29). But what did you do after you prayed? Is your heart just as heavy as before you prayed? Ask for forgiveness for your disbelief, and ask the Lord if, through His Holy Spirit, He will teach you how to pray and teach you to unpack your case of worries. He cultivates faith and trust in your heart. He will also show you that nothing is too big for His omnipotence or too small for His love.

There are people who trust the Lord for their eternal salvation but not for the worries of every day. They do not see that our problems are the material God intends to use to build a miracle. God loves you! Imagine a little girl going to her father with a broken doll. The little one is crying with grief. What does the father do? Does he say, "That old doll's not worth a cent, throw it away?" Of course not. He takes the doll and tries to repair it. Why does a grown man take such an old doll seriously? Because he sees it through the eyes of that little girl, whom he loves so much. Your heavenly Father sees your problem through your eyes because He loves you.

I like to tell of an experience I had when I was in prison. I had a cold and did not have a handkerchief. I told my sister Betsie, and she said, "Pray for a handkerchief." I started to laugh. Betsie prayed, "Father, I pray in Jesus' name that you will give Corrie a handkerchief because she has a cold." Just a bit later, I heard my name being called. I went to the window and saw a friend of mine who was also a prisoner and who worked in the hospital. "Here," she said, "take this, I am bringing you a present." I opened the package. It was a handkerchief! "How did you know that I needed a handkerchief? Did you know I had a cold?" "No," she said, "I was sewing handkerchiefs from an old piece of sheet, and a voice in my heart said, 'Take a handkerchief to Corrie ten Boom.'"

Can you understand what a handkerchief meant to me at that moment? That handkerchief, made of an old piece of sheet, was a message from heaven for me. It told me that there was a heavenly Father who listens when one of His children on planet earth prays for an impossibly small thing—a handkerchief. That same heavenly Father says to one of His other children, "Take a handkerchief to Corrie ten Boom." Isn't that wonderful? That is something Paul calls "the foolishness of

God," which is so much wiser than the wisdom of man. Read about it in 1 Corinthians 1–2.

Does God answer our prayers? Often, but not always. Why? Because He knows what we don't know. He knows everything. When we get to heaven, we'll thank God for all the answered prayers, but it may be that we will thank Him for the unanswered prayers even more because, then, we will be able to see things from God's perspective. We will see that God never makes mistakes.

Shall we pray? "Thank You, Father, that You love us so much and that we, if we are Your children, will one day see that. Will You teach us through Your Holy Spirit to bring our worries to You and leave them with You? Give us great faith to accept unanswered prayers and see that nothing can separate us from Your ocean of love in Christ Jesus our Lord. Hallelujah. Amen."

Eight

Are Unanswered Prayers God's Mistakes?

I am going to tell you something about so-called unanswered prayers. First of all, unanswered prayers are not evidence that God makes mistakes but, rather, that God knows what we do not know. God knows everything. I was in a concentration camp with my sister Betsie, and she became very sick. I took her to a hospital in the camp, and when she was in bed she said, "Will you pray with me for the Lord to heal me? Corrie, the Lord Jesus said, 'In My name you can lay on hands and they will be healed.' Will you do that?"

I prayed for her. We both believed that Betsie would be healed. The next morning I looked through the hospital window and saw them lifting Betsie's dead body from the bed to take it to the crematorium. That was the darkest hour of my life.

A couple of days later, I was unexpectedly released, probably because of a human error, but definitely through one of God's miracles. When I got to the office to sign out, I realized that they didn't know that Betsie was dead. It occurred to me to find out what would have happened to Betsie if she had not died. I asked, "Is my sister being released too?" The answer was,

"No, she is staying here for the duration of the war." "Can I stay with her?" I asked. The man became furious. "Get out, you are leaving immediately," he ordered.

Immediately, I saw God's perspective of the events. Just imagine that Betsie had gotten better and that I had had to leave her in that terrible camp and go to Holland alone.... I praised God and thanked Him for that unanswered prayer. I knew that Betsie was now in her Father's house with its many mansions. I knew that she couldn't be happier and that life couldn't be more glorious for her.

I therefore dare to expect that one day we will praise God and thank Him for all answered prayers, but even more so for the so-called unanswered prayers. A wise mother and father do not give their children everything they ask for. They know, better than the children, what is good for each child. This is not always understood. In countries in which communism reigns, Christians are often persecuted. When I told those Christians that Christians in Holland were faithfully praying for them, they were very appreciative, but not one person ever asked me, "Will you ask our brothers and sisters in Holland to pray that the persecution here will cease?" No, the request was always, "Will you ask them to pray that God will give us strength and courage to endure persecution?" May I ask you to faithfully pray for your brothers and sisters who are living in countries where they are persecuted and oppressed?

What does Paul say about prayer, both answered and unanswered? The text in Philippians is very clear: "Do not be anxious about anything, but in everything, by prayer and petition, with thanksgiving, present your requests to God" (4:6). "And my God will meet all your needs according to his glorious riches in Christ Jesus" (4:19). Did Paul experience that? Yes. But in verse 12 he writes, "I know what it is to be in need, and I know what it is to have plenty." He surely must have begged God for food when he was hungry, but he accepted unanswered prayer with this attitude: "I can do everything through him who gives me strength" (4:13). If you bring your requests to God through prayer and supplication, "The peace of God, which transcends all understanding, will guard your hearts and your minds in Christ Jesus" (4:7). The Holy Spirit allowed Paul to see circumstances from God's perspective.

Paul speaks about persecution, hardship, and famine in Romans 8:35–39. Nothing can separate us from the love of Christ? No! In all these things we are more than conquerors through Him who loved us. Nothing can separate us from the love of God that is in Christ Jesus our Lord. If something extremely serious happens, we can be confident that the best, the very best, is yet to come!

In New Zealand I met a boy, Chris L., who had so seriously injured his neck in an accident that he was almost completely paralyzed. Fortunately, his brain was not damaged. He was able to read and type, and had helped me correct a book that I had written. We became good friends. I perceived, however, that he could not accept that the Lord might not heal him. I spoke a lot to him and prayed with him so that he would surrender his suffering to God. I slept in the room next to his because he often needed help during the night. One night I could hear that he was awake, and I knew that there was a battle going on in his heart. I heard him cry out, "Oh God, make me willing to surrender everything to You!" The next morning I saw an expression of great joy and peace on his face. Chris has now become an assistant pastor, and I know he is a blessing to many.

Jesus' death on the cross seemed to be a total fiasco, but there He fulfilled everything necessary to save and redeem you and me. He carried our sins and pain. That is why it is possible for us to bring our so-called unanswered prayers to Him and to surrender them into the hands of Him who carried our problems and unanswered prayers on the cross. Yes, hallelujah, Jesus carried our pain, and His work is complete.

Shall we pray? "Thank You, Lord Jesus, that You have brought us to the ocean of God's love and that nothing can separate us from it. Thank You that Your Holy Spirit allows us to see circumstances from Your perspective so that we do not need to fear, even if the earth were to give way and the mountains were to move into the heart of the sea, as the psalmist says. Hallelujah. What a Savior! Amen."

Nine

Intercession

It is wonderful to be called to be intercessors. Anyone can do it! Do you know that not one of your prayers for someone else is lost? Not a single one. We sometimes forget that. The devil laughs at our plans. He smiles if we are up to our ears in work, but he trembles when we pray.

When I was five, I asked the Lord Jesus into my heart. The Lord made me an intercessor immediately!

First Timothy 2:1–3 says, "I urge, then, first of all, that requests, prayers, intercession and thanksgiving be made for everyone—for kings and all those in authority, that we may live peaceful and quiet lives in all godliness and holiness. This is good, and pleases God our Savior, who wants all men to be saved and to come to a knowledge of the truth."

Intercession is important work. Do you know that Isaiah 59:16 says that God was amazed that there was no intercessor? I remember that my sister Betsie and I were once in a Dutch concentration camp in Vught. We were there because we had rescued Jews. One day we thought that we were being called to be released, but, instead, we found ourselves standing in the middle of the concentration camp in front of a bunker that was being used as the jail. Standing to our right and left were prisoners. As we stood there, we realized that we might all be killed.

Suddenly, we noticed that there were no longer any guards. One of the prisoners shouted out, "Is there anyone here who can pray?" Betsie answered, "Yes, I can pray and I will." And she prayed! She prayed for herself, she prayed for the men next to her, she prayed for me, and she thanked the Lord that, even if we were killed, the best was yet to come for those who belonged to the Lord Jesus. She asked the Lord to take our hand if we were about to pass through the valley of the shadow of death. I can't remember what else she prayed, but it was a wonderful prayer. How marvelous it is to intercede.

Some time ago I was in Cuba with my assistant, Ellen de Kroon. It was difficult to work there; sometimes it was even very dangerous. Once I prayed, "Oh Lord, please tell our friends in Holland to pray for us." I do that quite often, and it is just as if I am sending them a telegram via headquarters: heaven. I feel so safe because I know my friends are praying for me.

When I returned to Holland, a girl came up to me—a very simple girl, not intellectual—but she loved the Lord Jesus very much. She approached me and said, "Auntie, on the 10th of April, you were in danger, weren't you?" I asked, "What makes you say that?" She said, "I woke up in the middle of the night, and the Lord said to me, 'Will you pray for Corrie?' And I did." That was precisely the moment I had asked for prayer! And you know, for that girl it was just as wonderful.

If you are an intercessor, you are in direct contact with the Lord. You are in the service of the King of kings. A while ago, I spoke in a large Australian church about the wonderful text of Revelation 3:20, in which the Lord Jesus says, "Here I am! I stand at the door and knock. If anyone hears my voice and opens the door, I will come in . . ." The Lord Jesus is speaking not only to people who know Him and love Him, but also to people who do not know Him or love Him. When He knocks, He listens to see if we say, "Yes." Even if we know Him, we often have to say, "Yes, Lord Jesus, come in." Do you know that the people in Laodicea to whom the Lord was speaking were Christians? They went to church, but something was missing: Jesus stood outside the door of their hearts.

I spoke to the people there in Australia and said, "It is so glorious that everybody may know that Jesus is knocking at the door of your heart. If you say, 'Yes,' He will come in." Afterwards I gave a kind of invitation: "If you said, 'Yes,' for the first time to the Lord Jesus, come up to the front and go to the room behind me. We'll pray for you there, give you some literature and explain to you what it means to have asked the Lord Jesus into your heart for the first time."

The first to come were two small girls. One of them asked me, "Am I too small to ask Jesus to come into my heart?" I said, "Why no, you're not too small. I was five when I asked the Lord into my heart, and He came—and He has never, ever deserted me. He has always stayed. That's a long time ago. The Lord Jesus is even interested in sparrows, and you are much bigger than a sparrow." Then the little girl said, "Lord Jesus, I have been very naughty, but will You please come into my heart and make it clean, cleanse it completely with Your blood. Amen."

Oh, it was so marvelous. Everyone heard what the little girl said. I am sure that the Lord came, just as He will come into your heart if you say, "Yes." I said to the other little one, "Would you like to do it, too?" She said, "I already did, a fortnight ago, and since then I've been praying for Mary every day, and now Mary did it." I said, "Then you must pray together for a third girl."

They looked at each other and at the same moment, they both said, "Anna." I said, "Then Anna it must be." They promised to pray for Anna, and when Anna had asked the Lord Jesus into her heart, then they could pray together for a fourth girl.

Intercession entered the hearts of the two little girls. Intercession can begin in your heart too. Surely you know someone who does not know the Lord. Pray for them and share the Gospel with him or her. Keep praying, and if the other person says, "Yes," pray together for a third person. Intercession can be the salvation of many people. Oh, if everyone would do it now, there would be a great revival in many countries.

Shall we pray? "Lord, will You use me? Will You use me as an intercessor? Thank You that I may intercede for others! Will You start a chain reaction of intercession in my heart, so that I can pray for another person, and then we can pray together for a third person, and then the three of us can pray for a fourth person? Thank You, Lord, that You want to use me! Hallelujah! Amen."

Ten

How Do We Prepare
for Jesus' Return?

I laid down my worries and looked at them. Part of them, I noticed, belonged to the past and another part to the future. Then I read in the Bible, "Each day has enough trouble of its own" (Matt. 6:34).

In my book about my life called *The Hiding Place*, I tell about an experience I had as a little girl. It was the first time I had seen a dead child. I had never encountered death before, and I became terribly worried—not just about my own death, but also that those whom I loved might die. I told my father about my fears. "Daddy, I am afraid that I will never be brave and strong enough to be a martyr for Jesus." He asked me, "If you go on a train journey from Haarlem to Amsterdam, when do I give you the ticket, three weeks ahead of time?" "No, Daddy, the day I am traveling," I replied.

"Right," said father, "and that's what God does too. You don't need a ticket now. You don't need the strength yet to suffer persecution for Jesus or to bear the death of people you love. But when the time comes, the Lord will give you the ticket right on time, all the strength and grace and courage you need." That comforted me very much, and often if I am worrying about the future, I think of my father's illustration and say to myself, "No, God has not given me the ticket yet, but I don't need it right now!"

Everyone who pays attention to world events, which we understand as signs of the time that Jesus may return very soon, can almost become scared at what the Bible says about the time of the Antichrist and the terrible things that will happen then. The moment will also come when we must all stand before a righteous God.

To be prepared, we need many promises that are in the Bible. We have to absorb them. Do you understand what I mean? Every promise of God's in the Bible is in Jesus. "Yes and Amen." And I notice—and I believe this is very clear in the Bible—that the Lord Jesus Himself wants to make us ready for that great day, when we will see Him face to face. I am so much looking forward to His return, aren't you?

Why do we look forward to it? Because we love Him. But He loves us much more than we love Him. That's why I believe that He is looking forward to it much more than we are! We understand that we have to be ready upon His return—completely ready. Whoever has this hope cleanses himself, as He is clean.

But then so often we try and we fail. It doesn't work. Even if I do my utmost to be pure and holy, and to walk in a good relationship with God and people, I still experience the temptations of the enemy. I think the enemy is very active at the moment in attacking God's children. He knows that time is very short.

How can you and I be prepared? Not by trying and trying again; that can be a victory for devout people who live by the flesh. They think they are so good—a great victory for the devil. But the answer to being prepared is this: Surrender yourself to

Him who wants you so much and who is prepared to make you ready for His return. First Thessalonians 3:12 says, "May the Lord make your love increase and overflow for each other and for everyone else, just as ours does for you."

Jesus doesn't only want to save us from our sins, but He wants to restore the image of God in us. We cannot summon up that love, but that's not necessary either. If we place our weak hand in the strong hand of the Lord, then He does it. He himself makes His love abundant. The Bible also says, "May he strengthen your hearts so that you will be blameless and holy in the presence of our God and Father when our Lord Jesus comes with all his holy ones" (1 Thess. 3:13).

"Blameless and holy." No, we cannot do that, we cannot become like that by trying, but He can do it! First Thessalonians 5:23 says, "May God himself, the God of peace, sanctify you through and through. May your whole spirit, soul and body be kept blameless at the coming of our Lord Jesus Christ."

How can that be? Blameless! Holy! Such words can just make us frightened when we look at ourselves. But, if we look to the Lord, we have no need to be afraid because the last part of this text is, "The one who calls you is faithful and he will do it." What will He do? He will give you and me the ticket we need for our journey.

What is that ticket? Not until then shall we fully understand (we understand it just a little bit now) that on the cross at Golgotha, Jesus fulfilled everything that was needed to prepare us for the future. Jesus said, "It is finished." If we look to the cross at Golgotha then we know: He is faithful, who did it and will do it. It is He who calls us. What you and I have to do is place our weak hand in His strong hand, surrender to Him, and then walk with Him through life. He wants to hold on to our hand with strength and accompany us on the narrow path. Do you know that wonderful song? We ourselves are weak, but in Him we are strong. In Him, who said that He will make us more than conquerors. So we need not fear the future. He will accompany us on the narrow path.

"Thank You, Lord, that we do not need to worry, but that You will guide us, even in these very difficult times. And not only that, Lord; You want to make us Your witnesses in a world in which there is so much darkness. Will You make us the light of the world? Thank You, Lord. Amen."

Eleven

God Prepares Us

What a world we live in! I find the news broadcasts so terrible that reading newspapers and listening to the news can make me despondent and sometimes almost desperate. We cannot see the final outcome, and often we become frightened as to where all this bad news will lead.

What a comfort it is to read the Bible and to see that God has long known what is happening now and that He has promised us a wonderful future in spite of all these terrible events that are occurring. In His words of farewell in Luke 21, the Lord Jesus described what we are now reading about in the newspapers.

That puzzling book, the Revelation of John, is much easier to understand now than it was ten or twenty years ago. There are terrible things prophesied in that book, but John saw the divine perspective. In Revelation 21:4 he says, "He will wipe every tear from their eyes. There will be no more death or mourning or crying or pain, for the old order of things has passed away." If we read the news reports we say, "The worst is yet to come." If we read the Bible we can cry out, "The best is still to come!" Jesus promised, "I am coming," and "I make all things new." Then this world, this dark world, will be covered with the knowledge of the Lord as the waters cover the sea.

If you read God's blueprint of world history, you are secure in the knowledge that God has plans for this world, and not problems. There has never been panic in heaven! The Lord Jesus said to watch out for the signs of the times. If we do that, then we know that He will return soon.

How can we be prepared? By surrendering to Him, of whom Paul said in Philippians 1:6, "I . . . being confident of this, that he who began a good work in you will carry it on to completion until the day of Christ Jesus." Here we see that on our side it is not a battle, not striving, not struggling, but surrendering.

The Lord Jesus wants to prepare us for His return. He loves us. He desires us more than we long for Him. In 1 Thessalonians 5:23–24 we read, "May God himself, the God of peace, sanctify you through and through. May your whole spirit, soul, and body be kept blameless at the coming of our Lord Jesus Christ. The one who calls you is faithful and he will do it." Just think what that means: you and I, blameless in spirit, soul, and body. That is possible because He who calls you is faithful. He will do it! Place your weak hand in His strong hand. He is faithful and He will do it.

Shall we pray? "Thank You, Lord Jesus, that You want to prepare us for Your return. Thank You that You have so clearly shown us the blueprint for world events in Your Word and that we know that if we, the branches, are connected to the vine, that in these difficult times we can produce fruits of peace, love, and comfort. Hold us tight. Amen."

Twelve

God Comforts Us

At the moment it is very dark in our world. The Lord Jesus told us that if we belong to Him, we are the light of the world. How much that is needed now!

Is that possible in a time like this? Yes, it is possible. I have experienced it myself. There was a time in my life when it was so dark that I said, "It has never been so bad and it can't get any worse." I was weak, and there was bitterness and fear in my heart instead of light. I had known the Lord Jesus for a long time, and I knew that I could find shelter with Him. I was with my sister, Betsie, in jail, prisoners of people who had been trained in cruelty. Everything was dark and awful.

Then Betsie and I started talking about the Lord Jesus. We opened the Bible and read about the ocean of God's love, into which we could throw ourselves—completely into His loving arms. We read what Jesus said before He left, "My peace I give you" (John 14:27). We felt His love and peace, and we sang softly, "Safe in the Arms of Jesus." We were so happy, and that evening Betsie said, "Wasn't it a wonderful day? We learned so much from the Lord."

How had we experienced that, how had we come to that? We did what Jesus said: "Come to me, all you who are weary and burdened, and I will give you rest" (Matt 11:28). Jesus gave us rest and a happiness that passes beyond all understanding.

Paul had many miserable experiences of cruelty and imprisonment. He wrote in 2 Corinthians 1:3–4, "Praise be to the God and Father of our Lord Jesus Christ, the Father of compassion and the God of all comfort, who comforts us in all our troubles, so that we can comfort those in any trouble with the comfort we ourselves have received from God." We experienced that. We started comforting those around us. We could comfort others because the Lord had comforted us. He spoke through us to the people. We were channels of living water, as the Lord had promised.

Next to the prison barracks where we were, there was a barracks full of Gypsies. We saw them frequently, and I remember that we prayed a lot for them. You can achieve so much through intercession. We did not meet many of them, but some time ago when a Gypsy lady in Germany was asked if she knew Jesus, she said, "Yes, I found Him when I was in a concentration camp. There Corrie ten Boom led me to Him. I know that Jesus died for me on the Cross. He died there for the whole world and for me too." You see, I had comforted her with the comfort God had given me.

In Luke 21:13 and 28, Jesus describes our times: "This will result in your being witnesses to them. . . . When these things begin to take place, stand up and lift up your heads, because your redemption is drawing near." You see, the Lord Jesus saw everything from God's perspective. He also sees everything that happens now from God's perspective.

God's plan is described in the Bible. What comfort Jesus gives in Revelation 21:5–6, ". . . I am making everything new," and "To him who is thirsty I will give to drink without cost from the spring of the water of life." What riches for you and me! Even if things get much worse, the best is still to come!

Let us pray. "Lord Jesus, come quickly and do what You promised and make all things new! Comfort us and give us the wonderful experience of passing on that comfort to others. Hallelujah. Amen."

Thirteen

God Gives Us Love

What does a Christian have if it is dark in the world? Love! In Africa a man came to a meeting with bandaged hands. I asked him how he had been injured. He said, "My neighbor's straw roof was on fire; I helped him to put it out and that's how my hands were burned."

Later I heard the whole story. The neighbor hated him and had set his roof on fire while his wife and children were asleep in the hut. They were in great danger. Fortunately, he was able to put out the fire in his house on time. But sparks flew over to the roof of the man who had set the house on fire and his house started to burn. There was no hate in the heart of this Christian; there was love for his enemy and he did everything he could to put out the fire in his neighbor's house. That is how his own hands were burned.

I already told how I experienced that love once myself, when I met a man who had been very cruel to my sister and me. He told me that he had found the Lord Jesus and confessed all his sins and now he was asking my forgiveness. There was bitterness in my heart when I thought of all he had done, but suddenly I thought of Romans 5:5: ". . . God has poured out his love into our hearts by the Holy Spirit." I said, "Thank You Lord that Your love is in my heart." Then I could say, "I forgive you for everything."

I was so happy, because Jesus has said that if we do not forgive, then we will not be forgiven. I couldn't do it, but Jesus in me could. On the cross Jesus said, "Father, forgive them for they do not know what they are doing." Jesus on the cross was the solution to our problem. What love, that God's Son carried our sins.

The love of God has been poured out in our hearts by the Holy Spirit, who has been given to us (Rom. 5:5). The love of God is great and strong; yes, we can speak of an ocean of love. That love gives us the strength to forgive and even to love our enemies. That love is a source of power and victory during the most terrible crises of our life, but also in everyday life.

We live in a danger zone. Hate, bitterness, fear, darkness, and self-centeredness are growing in the world around us, and we live in the midst of it. Television brings world events into our living rooms. The world is sick, and the danger of infection is serious. The demon of fear is so terribly strong. Hate and anger can quickly fill our hearts.

Fortunately, there is armor available (we can read about it in Ephesians 6), and we need that armor, right up to the last moment of our lives. It is Jesus Himself; we in Him and He in us (John 15:5). That is the new man, and the new man does not sin. Read about it in 1 John 2.

How can it be that such hate and fear can suddenly enter our hearts? That's the old man, who shows himself, and that's when the battle comes. But in Jesus we are conquerors (Rom. 8:37). The Holy Spirit produces fruit in us. Galatians 5:22 says, "The fruit of the Spirit is love, joy, peace, patience, kindness, goodness, faithfulness, gentleness and self-control."

The Lord Jesus used the example of the vine and the branches. A branch that remains in the vine produces fruit. If we remain in Jesus, He produces fruit through us. Then love regains the victory in our heart!

What we must and can do is confess our sins to Jesus. He forgives and cleanses us, and in a cleansed heart there is room for the fullness of God's Spirit. Hallelujah!

Let us pray. "Thank You, Lord, that You want to pour out Your love in our hearts through the Holy Spirit to each person who confesses his sin to You and is cleansed by Your blood. Savior, it is so dark in this world. There is so much hatred. Will You fill us with Your love so that we can pass it on to the poor people around us who are going through difficult times, when there is so much hate and fear? Keep us close to Your heart so that we, as branches of the vine, can produce the fruit of love. Thank You, Lord. Amen."

Fourteen

God Gives Us Security

What does a Christian have when it is dark in the world? Security!

In Colossians 3:3 we read, "hidden with Christ in God." It couldn't be safer! I sometimes show my hands as an example. I put my left hand over my thumb, and then I put my right hand over my left hand. You are the thumb. Jesus is the hand over your thumb; the right hand around it is God's—"hidden with Christ in God."

Some time ago I went to Japan. I went in obedience, but it was very difficult at first. I didn't know anyone, and in a country where you don't know the language, you have a strong sense of insecurity, especially if you are on your own. I opened my Bible and read 1 Peter 1:3–9, "Praise be to the God and Father of our Lord Jesus Christ! In his great mercy he has given us new birth into a living hope through the resurrection of Jesus Christ from the dead, and into an inheritance that can never perish, spoil, or fade—kept in heaven for you, who through faith are shielded by God's power until the coming of the salvation that is ready to be revealed in the last time. In this you greatly rejoice, though now for a little while you may have had to suffer grief in all kinds of trials. These have come so that your faith—of greater worth than gold, which perishes even though refined by fire—may be proved genuine and may result in praise, glory, and honor when Jesus Christ is revealed. Though you have not seen him, you love him; and even though you do not see him now, you believe in him and are filled with an inexpressible and glorious joy, for you are receiving the goal of your faith, the salvation of your souls."

What security! We are being kept for an inheritance; the inheritance is being kept for us. I saw this promise briefly from God's perspective. Things soon went really well in Japan. It was wonderful how the Lord opened hearts and doors for an exceptionally blessed ten months.

Obedience is extremely important. Love and obedience belong together. Even when it storms, there can still be peace. Jesus was obedient; He was prepared to die on a cross for you and me. What love!

In the center of a hurricane everything is quiet. I once experienced a hurricane in America. The storm passed just above us. It seemed as if we were in the middle of the storm; all about us was a raging wind. Heavy trees hit the ground and suddenly everything was quiet; nothing moved. The man sitting next to me said, "We are in the middle of the hurricane. It's quiet." It was only a brief moment; then the next half of the hurricane came. The real peace came when the storm had passed completely.

If we are hidden with Jesus in God, then peace remains. We are not afraid, even if the earth gives way and the mountains fall into the heart of the sea (Ps. 46:2). Even if it is night, we can experience the promise that "He who dwells in the shelter of the Most High will rest in the shadow of the Almighty" (Ps. 91:1). Hallelujah, what a sure security!

Shall we pray? "Thank You, Lord Jesus, that You give us certainty in the midst of uncertainty. Thank You that we are hidden with You in God. Listen, Lord, to those who now surrender to You. How marvelous that he, that she, is safe in Your arms. Amen."

Fifteen

How Can I Know What God Wants of Me?

We read in Isaiah 30:21, "Whether you turn to the right or to the left, your ears will hear a voice behind you, saying, 'This is the way; walk in it.'" Is that really true? Does God really lead His children?

Today I want to talk to you about what the Holy Spirit has to say to us about guidance, because that is often a problem for many people—sometimes for me too. There are many who say, "I never hear anything when I ask for guidance." But then I ask myself, Are you listening? Sometimes we have to wait on the Lord. But waiting in itself can be a blessing, if we do it in the presence of the Lord. That's what our "quiet time" is so good for.

If you are spiritually confused and you want to hear God's voice clearly, remain in His presence until the confusion changes. Much can happen during a time of waiting on the Lord. He sometimes changes pride to humility and doubt to faith and peace; yes, and even sometimes desire into purity. The Lord can and will do that. We must understand that sometimes the Lord's silence is His way of teaching us to grow, just as a mother calmly allows her child to fall and stand up again. If God sometimes allows conflicts, it may be His way of training us.

Some people say, "Oh, but it's very selfish to ask God for guidance." Do you know who whispers that to them? It is the enemy. The devil is terribly afraid of children of God who safely walk in the Lord's hand. It is God's will to guide us. Let's look at what the Bible says about His guidance: "I will instruct you and teach you in the way you should go; I will counsel you and watch over you" (Ps. 32:8). Could it be any clearer? And in Psalm 48:14, "For this God is our God for ever and ever; he will be our guide even to the end." Yes, it is God's will to lead us.

How come we so often do not hear the voice of the Lord? I believe it is because our sins are a barrier between Him and us. As the Psalmist says, his sins prevented him from looking up. Satan's work is sometimes like a mist on the outside of the window of our souls that hides the light of God. Our sinful desire is like the dirt on the inside of the window. Occasionally God puts His hand on the window; then He is very close by. If you don't receive guidance or hear the voice of God, the reason is often disobedience.

When I left a concentration camp during the war, I said (I will never forget this), "Now I want to travel over the whole world. I'll go wherever God leads, but one thing: I hope He never sends me to Germany." From my experiences in prisons I had a wrong, false picture of Germany. That was no surprise. I was therefore only partially obedient—anywhere Lord, but not Germany. I went to America, and I asked for guidance, but I didn't receive an answer. That was terrible! I asked the Lord, "Lord, is there maybe some sin between You and me?" I received a very clear answer: "Germany." I repented before the Lord and said, "Lord, then I'll go to Germany too."

I went to Germany, and I actually found that nowhere in the world were there as many open doors as in Germany. My best friends live there, but I also found my enemies there. I learned that if you love your enemies, you touch the ocean of God's love as never before. I'd learned my lesson: obedience! Not "Yes, but . . . ," but "Yes, Father." Peter said, "No, my Lord." But you can't say "no" if you say "My Lord," and you can't say "My Lord" if you say "no." It is most important to be obedient, because disobedience can make everything very dark.

God leads in three ways. First in our prayers, then through His Word (the Bible), and then through circumstances. It is so wonderful that in prayer, we don't only have the privilege of speaking to God, but of listening to Him, as well. That doesn't happen immediately; you have to get used to it. As Job says, "Submit to God and be at peace with him" (Job 22:21). In hidden companionship with God, we learn to hear His voice.

It is the devil who holds us back so that we cannot hear God's voice—that is his purpose. There are two rivals for God's voice, namely, yourself and the devil. We have to learn to differentiate between these voices.

God's commandments—His words—are simple, pure, and true, but those of the devil are complicated. He uses doubt, rebellion, and lies. Compare the following two voices. In Genesis 2:16–17 God says, "You are free to eat from any tree in the garden; but you must not eat from the tree of the knowledge of good and evil. . . ." Then we read what Satan says in Genesis 3:1: "Did God really say, 'You must not eat from any tree in the garden'?" You see, Satan twists God's words; and see how Satan loves to argue. Eve fell for it and began to argue too. Another difference is that Satan is always in a hurry, but God has time because He has eternity. His commands can often come very suddenly, but He always allows time to work them out.

It is not hard for the Lord to lead, and, therefore, asking God for guidance gives you a wonderful opportunity for hidden companionship with Him. It is such a comfort to know that before we were born, God had already made His plan for us. He gave us gifts and qualities, and He will surely not waste them now that you are a Christian! He, our good Shepherd, knows your physical, emotional, and spiritual needs better than you do. He said, "I will never leave you nor forsake you" (Josh. 1:5). He knows the end from the beginning and can allow all that you do and experience work for the good of yourself and others, if only we could better understand what it means to be a child of God.

When you accept God as your Savior, He, your Redeemer and Lord, makes you a child of God. If you have not done that yet, I hope that you accept Him now. But we have to understand what it means to be a child of God. God is our Father, who loves us. We are a part of Him. It is not hard work for Him to lead us; He thinks it's wonderful, and there is nothing too great for His omnipotence and nothing too small for His love.

Prayer: "Oh Father, we thank You that we are Your children and that You are a good Shepherd. Teach us through Your Spirit to hear Your voice clearly. Thank You. Hallelujah. Amen."

꒰

Sixteen

God's Guidance

Today I want to speak again about guidance and answer this question: May you ask God for a sign? Yes, I think so! Gideon asked for a sign, and he received it. Often God confirms what He has already said to His obedient child through a sign. You must be sure, however, that you ask with the right motive—not, for example, with the intention of seeking a shortcut to getting your own way or ending your quiet time more quickly. Playing heads and tails is much quicker than praying and listening to God's voice.

When I worked in Germany shortly after the war, I lived in one building with about four hundred people, all refugees. It was terrible. I never felt the needs of postwar Germany so much as when I lived there with these people. After a while I was exhausted. In that period I received an invitation from America to speak at a student's club, InterVarsity Christian Fellowship, and I really wanted to go. But then I grew a little hesitant because if you really want something, it could be that you say rather superficially, "Well, that must be God's guidance to go."

I asked for a sign. I said, "Lord, if I get a free trip to America, that will be a sign for me that I may go to America. I will

also buy chairs for the refugees if you give me the money for it."
During that time I had about one hundred and sixty refugees
to take care of, and I had no money to buy chairs for them. My
friends said, "That means you won't be going to America." I
said, "Why not? God can perform a miracle. Surely He can give
me a free trip?"

I went to the Oostzee company in Amsterdam. I can still see
myself standing there amongst the sailors to sign on as a stewardess. The captain at the quay looked at me strangely when I
said what I had come for. He looked me up and down from
head to toe, and I am sure he thought, Now, that's a rather old
stewardess. He said, "Do you know that if you sign on as a stewardess on one of our cargo ships, you have to sign on for the
return journey on the same ship and you can stay in America for
ten days?" I said, "No, ten months." "Exactly," he said, "that's
what I thought. You're not coming for a job. You want to get to
America a bit cheaply." "Yes, that's right," I replied. He then
said, "That's out of the question!"

I think he saw that I was a bit disappointed. Then he asked,
"What's your name?" "Corrie ten Boom," I replied. He said, "Did
you write A Prisoner, and Yet . . .?" We had a nice conversation
about loving your enemies because he thought it very odd that
I had returned to Germany. He said, "I won't be the one who
prevents you from getting a free trip!" I got my trip and went to
America. As soon as I arrived in America, I received a donation,
and I used it to buy chairs for my refugees.

Yes, I do believe that we may ask for a sign, and it is often
like that, too, if you seek God's guidance. As a Good Shepherd,
He knows what His sheep need. He loves His sheep. He loves
you, more than the best earthly shepherd loves his sheep.

I had asked the Lord what my schedule should be for the coming year. The Lord told me very clearly that I should go to Vietnam. Now, I didn't like that at all; I found it quite difficult, but I waited. Then I went to a conference for evangelists in Berlin. There, Bob Pearce of World Vision approached me— the man who is always at the place of catastrophes and great need. He is an enormous blessing! When he saw me, the first thing he asked was, "Corrie, when are you going to come with me to Vietnam?" I said, "As soon as you ask me, I'll come." The same thing happened again, when I was working in Germany for the American Army. God blessed my time there, and I was enjoying it immensely. Then the Army chaplain said, "Why don't you go to Vietnam? There are 300,000 American soldiers there." I knew what to do.

You see, that's what it means to have the Lord guide us very clearly. He not only wants to lead us, but if we listen obediently and follow Him, then we are at peace. If you have an important decision to make, or even a small one, it is good to make your decision with the guidance of the Lord.

First, we have to check whether we are obedient to God's will; then we have to question our motives for wanting to go there or to do that. We can test our motives with the Bible. The Sermon on the Mount (Matt. 5–7) is a wonderful norm by which we can test our motives, as is 1 Corinthians 13, or whatever Scripture the Lord leads us to. Always make sure your decision is made in God's presence, when you are really together with Him. This will help you to better distinguish His voice and be certain of His blessing on your decision. It is a wonderful experience to discuss your plans with the Lord. You develop such a warm relationship with Him. He is a very, very Good

Shepherd. He loves us, and He delights in leading us. We have to realize that He loves to guide us.

I also wanted to talk about human advice. Yes, God also speaks through human advice, but we must be careful because often this can lead to confusion. Imagine if Samuel had asked people their opinions on who would make a suitable king of Israel. Do you think one person would have said, "Hey, the boy walking behind the sheep, you should choose him to be king?"

Human advice, by itself, can bring confusion. Often the best advice is offered by people who don't know themselves that they are being used by God. A church service, especially a prayer meeting, can be helpful—praying together with others and waiting together on God, first in silence and then praying aloud. The Lord Jesus wants to be our guide, when there is darkness around us, to light our path.

"Thank You, Lord Jesus, that You came and thank You that You are a friend who never deserts us. Lord, teach us by Your Spirit to better distinguish Your voice. Thank You that You want to do this. Thank You for Your great love. Thank You that You carried the sins of the whole world on the cross, and our sins in particular. Thank You that You have given us the answer to two great problems in our lives: the problem of sin and the problem of death. How You loved us; how You still love us. Thank You, Lord Jesus. Amen."

Seventeen

Going Where God Sends You

One morning I spoke in a church in Copenhagen, Denmark. The text was Romans 12:1 "I urge you, brothers, in view of God's mercy, to offer your bodies as living sacrifices, holy and pleasing to God—this is your spiritual act of worship." I told my audience that they had to give their bodies as a pleasing sacrifice to the Lord. I said that although I was an elderly woman, I still wanted to give myself completely to Jesus and do what He desired me to do and go where he desired me to go—to be obedient even to the point of death.

After the service, two nurses approached me. They invited me for a cup of coffee in their apartment. I was very tired. A cup of coffee seemed very appealing, and I gratefully accepted their invitation. But I was not prepared for the steep climb to their room. Many of the houses in Copenhagen are very old and have no elevators, and the nurses lived on the tenth floor. . . . "Oh Lord, I don't think I can make it," I said. But the nurses were so insistent that I should visit them that I didn't dare refuse. When I at last reached the fifth floor my old heart was beating heavily and my legs refused to go a step further. I saw a chair and sat down. I said to the nurses, "Go on to your room. When I've rested I'll come too."

I asked the Lord, "Why do I have to walk up so many flights of stairs after such a busy day, Lord?" The answer came immediately: "Because there will be such a great blessing up there. It will even give joy to the angels of God." I looked at the winding stairs, which I could see going on right to the top. "Maybe I am going to heaven," I thought, "that will give joy to the angels." I counted the steps. There were a hundred or more. But if God said that the work would make the angels rejoice, I had to go. I stood up and started to climb again. At last I reached the tenth floor, and when I arrived in the nurses' room, I found a table brightly laid. The meal had been prepared by the parents of one of the nurses. I knew that I only had a little time, and I knew too that in one way or another, God was going to give a blessing. So I soon started a conversation.

"Tell me," I asked the nurse's mother, "was it long ago that you got to know the Lord Jesus?" "I have never met Him," she said, a little surprised at my question. I said, "Don't you want to come to Him? He loves you. I have talked of Him in more than sixty countries, and I have never met anyone who regretted giving his heart to Jesus, and neither will you if you do."

I opened the Bible and read her texts that made salvation through the Lord Jesus very clear. She listened with great interest. Then I asked, "Shall we speak together with the Lord?" I prayed and both the nurses prayed with me. At last, the mother put her hands together and said, "Lord Jesus, I actually know a great deal about You. I just read the Bible, but I now pray for You to come into my heart. I need salvation and cleansing. I know that You died on the cross for the sins of the whole world and for my sin too. Please Lord Jesus, come into my heart and make me a child of God. Amen."

I looked up and saw tears of joy on the faces of the young nurses. They had prayed so much for the parents, and now their prayers had been answered. I turned to the father, who had quietly listened to everything. "What do you think of this?" I asked. "I have never made a decision for the Lord Jesus," he said seriously, "but I have listened to everything you said to my wife and I now know the way. I will pray to Jesus too, for Him to save me." He bowed his head, and from his lips came a joyful, serious prayer as he gave his life to Jesus Christ. I know that there were angels around us who were praising God. It says in the Bible that the angels rejoice over every sinner who repents.

"Thank You, Lord," I whispered, as I went down the many stairs, "that You let me walk up all these steps to the top. The next time, Lord, help Corrie ten Boom listen to her own sermons, so that I am ready to go where You lead, even if it is steps up to the tenth floor."

Let us pray together. "Lord, we thank You that You give us the willingness to go where You lead us, and we thank You that we stand on victory ground if we strive and work in obedience to You. We thank You that You in no way drive away those who come to You, but that You feel great joy when we place our lives in Your hands. Thank You for the people there in Denmark. Will You bless them, Lord; and will You bless us and make us a blessing. Hallelujah! Amen."

Eighteen

Have You Left Your First Love?

I recall an experience in Africa. It was during a sort of one-year holiday—a Sabbath year we called it. I had enjoyed living in a house where missionaries and others could rest. The house had a beautiful tropical garden overlooking Lake Victoria. The climate was tropical, but because of the altitude, it was not too warm. I very much enjoyed the rest, especially since I was able to sleep in the same bed every night. During the previous twenty years, I had slept in more than one thousand different beds.

I could work, fortunately—meetings in churches and universities, clubs and prisons—but not more than three or four times a week. Now the year of rest prescribed by the doctor was over. On November 1, I was free to leave. My assistant Connie and I laid all the invitations and a map of the world on the bed and asked God to guide us as to how we should prepare the coming program. We had grown accustomed to not making plans first and then asking God for His signature. No, we waited for guidance from the Lord first, and then we endorsed His plans.

It was a nice schedule. Four months more in Africa, two months in Eastern Europe, three months in America . . . but I didn't feel happy. Was it really necessary to travel again? I discussed it with the Lord. That's always good, if your heart is not completely happy with His guidance. "I want what You want, Lord. I want to work wherever You lead me, but there are plenty of opportunities here, in churches, clubs, and prisons." I felt so happy. Of course it was good in God's eyes—I wouldn't have to travel, and I could sleep in the same bed every night.

"You have a visitor," Connie called, "a brother from Rwanda." A black minister came up to me. "We are so happy that you are coming to Rwanda," he said. "Five years ago you visited us. You said then how the Lord Jesus had never let you down. Your stories were so good, but it didn't mean much to us. We had never been in prison. But a couple of years ago there was a war. Many, including me, went to jail and your stories of your experiences helped so much. That's why we are so happy you are coming back."

That was just what I didn't want! To change the subject somewhat, I asked some questions. "What kind of church do you have? What message do you think your people need?" Without a moment's hesitation the minister opened his Bible and read from Revelation 2: "To the angel of the church in Ephesus write: These are the words of him who holds the seven stars in his right hand and walks among the seven golden lampstands: I know your deeds, your hard work and your perseverance. I know that you cannot tolerate wicked men, that you have tested those who claim to be apostles but are not, and have found them false. You have persevered and have endured hardships for my name, and have not grown weary. Yet I hold this against you: You have forsaken your first love. Remember the height from which you have fallen! Repent and do the things you did at first. If you do not repent, I will come to you and remove your lampstand from its place." That was the message for Ephesus and for Rwanda. For Corrie ten Boom, too, was my echo!

How I had changed! Twenty years before, I had gotten out of jail, weak and ill, but I was interested in two important things. First, the salvation of souls. I could tell them about Jesus, about how He had accomplished on the cross everything that was necessary to redeem them from sin. I could tell them about the wonderful glory of being a child of God and invite them to come to Him. Secondly, I was interested in glorifying the Name of the Lord by talking about the special miracles I had experienced, about who the Lord Jesus was to me when I was in prison, and about how He had never let me down. Yes, that was twenty years ago; that's what I was interested in then. And now? I was interested in my bed!

I had forsaken my first love. I opened my Bible and read, "If you do not repent. . . ." (Rev. 2:5). There was such great joy in my heart. The door to repentance was wide open. I asked for forgiveness. The Lord forgave me and cleansed me with His blood. Hallelujah! I obeyed God's program, and what a blessing it was. Had I returned to my first love? No, much better than that. The Lord forgave me and cleansed my heart with His blood; He fills a cleansed heart with His Holy Spirit and His love (Rom. 5:5). His love, the fruit of the Spirit, is far more than my first love ever was. Have you forsaken your first love? I have a wonderful message for you. The door of repentance is wide open.

"Thank You, Lord Jesus, for the ocean of love that we can possess when You cleanse our hearts and fill them with Your Holy Spirit. Listen, Lord, to whoever now says, 'Savior, I have forsaken my first love. Forgive me, cleanse my heart, fill me with Your Spirit and Your love.' Thank You, Lord Jesus. Amen."

Nineteen

God Works Through Our Helplessness

once read in a newsletter that if we say that the Lord may use us, then we should not be surprised if we sometimes face impossible situations in life.

If we have given ourselves completely to the Lord, then He will show His greatness through our helplessness. We read in Luke 9 about the feeding of the five thousand. In verse 13 the Lord Jesus said to His disciples, "You give them something to eat," and verse 17 says, "They all ate and were satisfied, and the disciples picked up twelve basketfuls of broken pieces that were left over."

I was once in a country where there was much hatred. Divorce was prevalent; the streets were extremely dangerous, especially in the evenings. Murders were common. I heard about an old lady who was murdered for $10. I had a message for that country. I had experienced myself that if the Lord Jesus tells us to love our enemies, He gives us the love He asks of us (Rom. 5:5). I wanted to tell them, "Friends, you don't need to try yourself, you can't; but if you open your heart to the Lord

Jesus, then He will bring God's love into your heart through the Holy Spirit."

When the Lord clearly told me to visit that country, I encountered much opposition. "Stay in Holland," people said, "we don't need you here." I told them, "The Lord has guided me to come to this country." "Rubbish," answered the people, "that doesn't happen—guidance from the Lord, that's fanaticism."

Fortunately I was not discouraged. A little while ago, I went there again. I was asked to speak on television. One thing led to another and I spoke eight times in front of the big lamps that shone in my face, opposite cameras that broadcast my words and face to millions of people. Yes! I was able to tell four million people that the Holy Spirit brought love for my enemies into my heart.

I had hated the people who had put me, my family, and my friends in prison during World War II. Those people had on their consciences the death of my father, who, at the age of eighty-four, had died ten days after entering prison, and the death of my sister Betsie, who died after ten months of terrible suffering. But because the Holy Spirit had given me the love of God in my heart, I was able to forgive and love those same people I had hated!

I was eighty-one years old and could not travel very much, but God performed a miracle. Millions of people were able to hear my message. A mother wrote to me, "Now I can forgive the murderer of my eighteen-year-old daughter." She was one of the many people God reached by letting me speak on television. Feeding five thousand people with five loaves and two fishes—impossible! But Jesus said, "You give them something to eat," and the disciples obeyed, and a miracle took place: twelve baskets filled with pieces of food were left.

Do you have an impossible job to do? Has the Lord told you to do it? Go ahead! When we pray, we enter God's domain from the domain of our inability. He is conqueror and makes us more than conquerors. It is not bad if we feel weak, if our inability is a reality to us. That's exactly when the Lord does miracles. Paul said, "When I am weak, then I am strong." Do you know why I thought it so important that these people in that country learned to forgive? Jesus said that if we do not forgive, we will not be forgiven, and we break down the bridge that we need for ourselves. Jesus is coming again very soon, and we must be prepared—by being in good relationship with God and with others. We can't get it together ourselves, however hard we try. But if we place our weak hand in the strong hand of Jesus, then He does it. Jesus is looking forward to His return to earth and it is He who is preparing us for His return. Surrender to Him completely. He who began a good work in you will bring it to completion on that day—the day of His second coming.

Our family had a little savings box, and when it was full, it was given to missions. "A dime in the blessing box!" was my Mother's cry when kind, unexpected guests arrived. If we sold an expensive watch from our watchmakers' shop, if the Lord saved us from an accident just in the nick of time, or if we arrived home safely after a journey or camp, the blessing box was put on the table. Try it sometime! It accentuates our blessings wonderfully! You become doubly thankful for them. "Count your blessings, name them one by one, and it will surprise you what the Lord has done!"

Keep looking in the right direction in everything you do—that is so important. I often say, "Keep looking up and kneeling down." One day I met a missionary who was desperate because Christians were continually being killed near her home. "Look down on the storms and terrible events around us, down from on high," I said, "from the heavenly realms where Jesus' victory is the greatest reality." This is only possible through the Holy Spirit.

I remember from my time in prison in Ravensbrück, where so many men and women were killed, that Betsie and I sometimes walked in the prison grounds before we were called for registration in the mornings at 4:30 A.M. Then God performed a miracle. We experienced His presence so vividly that it was as if we were talking to one another. Betsie would say something, then I would say something, and then the Lord would say something—and both Betsie and I heard what He said. I cannot explain it, but it was wonderful. We saw then that even though everything was terrible, we could rely on the fact that God did not have any problems, only plans. There is never panic in heaven! You can only hold on to that reality through faith because it seemed then, and often seems now, as if the devil is the victor. But God is faithful, and His plans never fail! He knows the future. He knows the way.

Watchman Nee once said that surrender to the Lord means turning around one hundred and eighty degrees—that means a renewed person and renewed vision. Even John, the disciple whom Jesus loved, had to have his eyes on his eternal Lord (Rev. 1). We are not ready for the battle until we have seen the Lord, for Jesus is the answer to all problems.

Look to the Lord and you will gain His perspective on the difficulties. Second Corinthians 4:17–18 says, "For our light and momentary troubles are achieving for us an eternal glory that far outweighs them all. So we fix our eyes not on what is seen, but on what is unseen. For what is seen is temporary, but what is unseen is eternal." You don't understand? That doesn't matter. Just believe. Psalm 10:14 says, "But you, O God, do see trouble and grief; you consider it to take it in hand."

"Lord, keep us close to Your heart, so that we see everything in and around us from Your perspective. Then we will not fear because we know that You never make a mistake. Hallelujah. Amen."

Twenty

Reasons for Demon Possession

How is it that people become possessed by evil spirits or come under their influence? We can often find the reasons in occult sin. That is very clear and apparent with fortune-telling. In Deuteronomy 18:10–12 we read, "Let no one be found among you who sacrifices his son or daughter in the fire, who practices divination or sorcery, interprets omens, engages in witchcraft, or casts spells, or who is a medium or spiritist or who consults the dead. Anyone who does these things is detestable to the LORD, and because of these detestable practices the LORD your God will drive out those nations before you."

When I was working in Germany after the war, people often talked to me about not being able to pray. They could not concentrate when they read the Bible or listened to a sermon. They were often plagued by thoughts of suicide—a very clear indication that a demonic influence is present. I later discovered the reason. Just after the war, many men and boys in Germany were still missing. People didn't know if they were in a concentration camp in Russia or if they had died in battle. This uncertainty was awful, so people went to see fortune-tellers. Whether they got any correct information, I do not know, but this was the reason for the darkness that I later saw during my pastoral work there. The door had been opened to dark powers due to this sin. Usually it was not difficult to convince people that this is a sin in the eyes of the Lord. The Bible is very clear about this in Deuteronomy 18: it is an abomination in God's eyes because it is apparent that someone is asking for help from the enemy instead of trusting in God's power.

It was marvelous to explain to them how they could be set free (1 John 1:7, 9). I told them that if they knew that they had sinned, they could bring this sin to the Lord, confess it, and ask for forgiveness. I saw this promise become reality. The Lord forgave them and cleansed them with His blood and filled them with His Holy Spirit. The fruit of the Spirit is, among other things, peace and joy (Gal. 5:22)!

Taking part in spiritist experiments can also open the door to occult darkness. Very frequently, when I warn against fortune-telling and spiritism, I ask if people have taken part in it, and the answer I often get is, "I only did it for a joke," or "I didn't believe in it."

When I get this reply, I use this example. A while ago in Germany, before the wall had been built, half of the city was forbidden to West Berliners. Part of the border passed through a forest. If a West Berliner was caught playing in the forest on East German territory, he would be arrested. It would not help if he said, "I was only playing, or I did it for a joke." If you are on enemy territory, then you are in the enemy's power. The same applies when you jokingly commit occult sins.

Another very dangerous sin is to wear amulets. You cannot be too careful about this. I heard of a girl who was always sick.

Someone gave her an amulet to wear around her neck. The illness was immediately cured, but the child became very depressed. She never laughed. When she was twelve, she tried to commit suicide. An evangelist visited her and asked if she had an amulet. She gave it to him, but she begged him not to open it! Nevertheless, he opened it and found a piece of paper, on which was written, "I command you, Satan, to keep this body healthy until you have its soul in hell." They destroyed the amulet, and the child was freed, but immediately she became seriously ill. She was later cured by the laying on of hands in the name of Jesus.

Apart from fortune-telling and wearing charms and amulets, contact with false teachers or with people who exercise demonic influence (for example, palm readers, astrologers, or magnetic healers) can be a reason for darkness, as can reading horoscopes or occult books, experimenting with hypnotism, attempting to contact the dead, or carelessly associating with the sins of others or with demonized people. For good reason, Paul warns Timothy against hasty laying on of hands.

In Indonesia, where there was a great revival, it was common to see people surrender to the Lord, repent of their sins, and burn and destroy all idols, amulets, and occult books. As we live in such dangerous times, all compromise is an especially great threat. If we choose Jesus' side, we stand as children of light in the midst of a dark generation. But our choice must be very definite. What joy that there is forgiveness and salvation in Jesus.

Let us pray: "Dear Father, in Jesus' name we pray that You will allow us to clearly see if there is any compromise with Satan or his demons in our lives and hearts. Thank You that You want to free us and strengthen us, that You want to cleanse us with the blood of Jesus, Your dear Son, and strengthen us through Your Holy Spirit. Hallelujah! Amen."

Twenty-One

Victory Over Demons

What can we do if we meet others who are under the influence of, or possessed by, dark powers? In Jesus' name, we can cast out the demons. Fear of demons comes from the demons themselves. If we are hidden with Jesus in God, then we are safe. In Him we are strong. Read about it in John 15: He in us, we in Him! The Lord Jesus commands us to cast out demons; however, I would advise you not to do this on your own.

The first thing that should take place is that both parties who are to carry out this work must ask the Lord to search their hearts to see if there is any unconfessed sin in their lives. An unconfessed sin can be a point of contact for the devil and put us in danger. If the person who wishes to be freed is a child of God, then we can talk about this freely. If someone comes to us who desires to be freed and is aware of being under the influence of a demon, then everything is relatively simple. We must first pray for the protection of the blood of Jesus and then clearly speak to the evil forces IN THE NAME OF JESUS. Not in the name of Christ—that is His title. The name of Jesus is the Name above all names. His name has power. It is best to look straight into the eyes of the other person. You can and you must speak clearly to the demons and command them in Jesus' name to leave the person—not forgetting to forbid them to come back or enter another person. I say, "Go to the place God tells you to go."

We can then give thanks for the liberated person, but he or she must surrender completely to the Lord. After all, Jesus said that if the house is empty and clean, and it remains empty, other demons will come; and the latter state will be worse than the former state (Matt. 12:43–45). Now the heart of this person can be filled with the Holy Spirit by submission and confession of sin and through prayer for the fullness of the Spirit. What joy!

It is good for the person who has been released never to speak of the experiences he or she has had, other than to praise and thank the Lord. Those who were present should also never speak about these things. The urge for sensationalism is from the wrong quarters. Advise the person to read the Bible. Disciple them with texts such as, "He who began a good work in you will carry it on to completion until the day of Christ Jesus" (Phil. 1:6). Direct them to Jesus.

It is difficult if a person who is under the influence of demons is not aware of it. Then you need much wisdom; but as James 1:5 says, all the wisdom that we need has been promised to us. It is good in such cases to use the word "the enemy" or "the evil one" rather than demon or devil. Even if we are not present, we can do something—by claiming the promise in the Bible that whatever we bind on earth in the name of the Lord Jesus will be bound in heaven (See Matthew 16:19).

When I was in a concentration camp in the war and was confronted constantly with death, I found everything so simple. I saw myself and I saw the devil, and the devil was much stronger than I. But I saw Jesus too, and Jesus was much stronger than the evil one. Because I was on Jesus' side, I was more than conqueror! We must never forget that Jesus is always conqueror, and that we just need to be in the right relationship with Him; then His victorious life flows through us and touches others. We can never expect too much of the Lord. Hallelujah, what a Savior! Those who are with us are many more in number and much stronger than those who are against us. On our side stands a mighty High Priest with legions of angels.

One of the terrible consequences of the influence of demons is that the affected person cannot convert, even if he or she wants to! When the person has been released, you can tell him or her that the path is now open. Speak about conversion and tell them to put their weak hand in the strong hand of Jesus the Lord. Ask them to respond wholeheartedly to Revelation 3:20, in which Jesus says, "Here I am! I stand at the door and knock. If anyone hears my voice and opens the door, I will come in and eat with him, and he with me." This decision for the Lord Jesus makes the angels in heaven rejoice. Jesus gives those who accept Him the right to become children of God.

There are more angels than demons! A third of the angels fell, so if we work out the math, we can say that for every demon there are two angels. It is wonderful to know of the reality of angels. As it says in Hebrews 1:14, "Are not all angels ministering spirits sent to serve those who will inherit salvation?"

Read the story of Elisha's servant (2 Kings 6). It is wonderful to know that angels are a reality. Those who are with us are greater in number and stronger than those who are against us. I always find it marvelous to hear on the mission field how the enemy often sees angels, even if the believers don't see them at all.

In Africa, enemies surrounded a mission school to murder the children. They approached three times, but each time they turned back and disappeared. One of them was wounded and was helped by a mission doctor who asked him, "Why didn't you force your way into the school?" The man replied, "We couldn't because there were so many soldiers there in white uniforms."

The Vietnamese had a similar experience when the Viet Cong attacked a village of sixteen hundred people to murder them. All the Christians went to the church and prayed constantly. The enemy saw angels around the village, which caused them to retreat. We do not need to see angels, but we know that they are there because we have the Word of God.

Let us pray: "Father, we thank You in Jesus' Name that there are so many of Your servants around us to protect us. How wonderful it will be to see them in heaven, but what a blessing that they protect us now. Thank You for Your continuing protection and love. Teach us by Your Spirit to believe Your Word about all the riches that are available to us. Teach us to accept them, and teach us how to use them. Thank You that those who are with us are stronger and greater in number than those who are against us. Thank You that You are with us, Lord Jesus, until the end of the world. Hallelujah, what a Savior! Amen."

Twenty-Two

The Courage of Faith

few years ago, I was in a country far from here, and I had to speak on a Sunday morning in church. When I looked at the people, I could see fear written all over their faces. You could feel the tension. No wonder. Every day during the previous week, a large number of Christians had received a piece of paper telling them to report to the police. At night they heard shooting in the beautiful sports stadium just outside the town. All those who reported were shot. That happened every day; each time more Christians.

I didn't understand the political background at all, but I did know that there was a new government. As I was sitting in the church, I saw people looking at each other anxiously. I could easily understand what they were thinking: Will he be killed this week? Will she still be alive next week? Will I still be here?

I asked the Lord for a word from the Bible to give to these people. The Lord gave me 1 Peter 4:12–14: "Dear friends, do not be surprised at the painful trial you are suffering, as though something strange were happening to you. But rejoice that you participate in the sufferings of Christ, so that you may be overjoyed when his glory is revealed. If you are insulted because of the name of Christ, you are blessed, for the Spirit of glory and of God rests on you."

"If you have to suffer and maybe die for Jesus soon," I said to the people, "then He will ensure that you have all the courage and grace that you need in time. Don't be afraid. Don't forget that there is a crown in heaven for all martyrs. The Spirit of God, the Spirit of glory, will rest on you, says Peter."

There was great joy in the church. When the service was over, someone began to sing, "In the sweet by and by, we shall meet at the beautiful shore. . . ." The people kept singing that song as they left the church, and I heard that song for quite some time as they walked down the road. I soon found out that roughly half of those people in the church were killed that week.

At midnight, we could hear shooting continually. We worked in a kind of radio studio there. One morning we had a meeting in the building. It was well insulated against sound from outside. When we left the building after the meeting, there were groups of people on the street. "What happened?" we asked. "Didn't you hear? There was a storm, and lightning hit the stadium, right where the gunpowder and weapons were kept. The whole building was blown up. That was God's judgment for killing the Christians."

Some time ago I was at a large international evangelists' congress in Lausanne. I met people from many countries, including a missionary from the country where these events had taken place. I asked, "How are things going with your radio station?" "Oh, wonderful. The studio was closed for a year, and now we have permission to broadcast again. Day and night the gospel is heard on all sides." "That's wonderful," I replied, "and tell me, how are the friends I worked with?" She waited for a minute. Then she said, "They were all killed." She saw how shocked I was. She put her hand on my shoulder and said, with a smile on her face, "They were promoted ahead of us."

Yes, the Spirit of glory rested on them. I saw it from God's side. If you are close to the Lord, then you can see things from His side—a bird's-eye view from heaven. Then you can smile, even when you speak of terrible things that have happened.

That is what you and I need—to see things from God's perspective. Then we know that He does not make mistakes, and that our present suffering is worth nothing compared to the glory that is to come. God works out His plan on earth. Even if we go through great trials and the trials are, perhaps, even deeper than we experience now, we can know that the best is yet to come! That is a great comfort.

"Thank You, Lord, that You always give Your courage and strength in time, even if we have to suffer and perhaps die for You. Allow us through Your Holy Spirit to always see things from Your perspective, because then we need not fear, even if the earth gives way and the mountains fall into the sea. Thank You, Lord! Amen."

Twenty-Three

Are You Afraid of Death?

There is a story of two monks who said to one another, "Whoever dies first has to come back and tell the other what heaven is like." One died and came back to the other the next day and said two words, "Totaliter aliter," that is, "totally different." The Bible says that too: "No eye has seen, no ear has heard, no mind has conceived what God has prepared for those who love him" (1 Cor. 2:9).

The Bible says that man is destined to die once and, after that, to face judgment. So if we know it's coming, we ought to prepare for it. I am not frightened of death. "How can you be so sure?" you might ask. My reply is that I know death. I've looked into its eyes, not occasionally, but steadily for a few months when I was in a barracks in a concentration camp that looked out onto a crematorium. Every day about six hundred bodies were burned—the bodies of prisoners who died or were killed. When I saw the smoke from the chimney of the crematorium, I asked myself, "When will it be time for you to be killed?" I didn't know then that a few weeks before prisoners of my age were to be killed, I would be released miraculously. I noticed then that I was not afraid. Perhaps you are thinking,

"What courage!" But it wasn't courage. It was the Lord Jesus who gave me security. The Bible says, "Where, O death, is your victory? Where, O death, is your sting?" (1 Cor. 15:55). I thank God for the victory of the Lord Jesus Christ. I know that about two thousand years ago the Lord Jesus bore my sins, and then He said, "It is finished." The answer is on the cross. The Bible sums it up so clearly: "If we confess our sins, He is faithful and just and will forgive us our sins and purify us from all unrighteousness" (1 John 1:9). Believe in the Lord Jesus and you will be blessed.

Many years ago, I talked at a girls' club about God's judgment—that Jesus is the Judge who judges us. Romans 8:34 was my text: ". . . Christ Jesus, who died—more than that, who was raised to life—is at the right hand of God and is also interceding for us."

Pietje Stevens, a particularly sweet girl, looked worried. Suddenly her face lit up. "Oh how wonderful," she said, "our judge is also our advocate." Jesus Christ, the Judge, at the right hand of God, is also the one who pleads for us. What a relief. It wasn't long after that I visited Pietje in the hospital. I'll never forget it. She was dying. "Pietje, do you know that our judge is also our advocate?" She whispered, "Thank You, Jesus."

The Bible says that the wages of sin is death. The grace that God gives is eternal life in the Lord Jesus Christ. When Pietje Stevens died, I looked at her and knew that she was safe with the Lord, who does not make mistakes.

Is everything okay with you? Do you know the Lord Jesus? Have you asked Him to live in your heart? Have you asked for forgiveness of your sins and said, "Thank You, Jesus, that You died at the cross for me? Thank You that I am forgiven?" Then you, too, can say, "Thank You that You will be the judge and also my advocate." Jesus says, "Come to Me, all of you," and that includes you.

"Oh, Lord Jesus, we thank You that You have such great love and that we may all come to You. Thank You for what You did on the cross, and what You will do as judge and advocate. Hallelujah! What a Savior. Amen."

Twenty-Four

What Is Your Final Destination?

I was once on a mission plane. That is always such a wonderful experience! In a large plane you forget that you are up high in the air but in a small plane you see the ground beneath you, the sky around you, and you feel really dependent on the Lord's protection. I asked the pilot, "Where are we going?" He answered immediately because he was in no doubt as to our destination.

I remember that I once had to order a plane ticket in the country formerly known as Formosa. It was a long itinerary: Formosa—Sydney (Australia)—Auckland—Sydney—Cape Town (South Africa)—Tel Aviv (Israel)—Amsterdam. The young lady in the office asked me, "What is your final destination?" "Heaven," I replied. "How do you spell that?" she asked. "H-e-a-v-e-n," I said. She wrote it under the word Amsterdam, but then she suddenly understood what I meant. "I don't mean that," she said. I remarked, "Oh no? But I do mean it, but you don't need to write it down, I already have my ticket." "What do you mean by that?" she asked. I explained, "About two thousand years ago, someone ordered my ticket to heaven. I just needed to accept it from Him. That was the Lord Jesus, when He bore the punishment for my sins on the cross."

A man from Formosa who was standing in front of us, turned around and said, "That's true." I asked him, "It's good you know that; do you have a reservation in heaven?" "I certainly do," he said. "I accepted Jesus as my Savior and He made me a child of God. Every child of God has a place reserved in the Father's house with its many mansions, where Jesus has prepared a place for all those who know Him as their Redeemer."

"Brother, come here," I said. "Miss, if you don't have a reserved seat in a plane, you can get into great difficulty; I've experienced that. But if you don't have a place reserved in heaven, you are in far deeper trouble. Brother, you must make sure your colleague isn't too late to make a reservation." Was that a joke? No, I was serious, and I'm serious when I ask you, "Are you sure you'll get to heaven when you die?"

If you are not sure, then I can give you a wonderful message. Come to Jesus. He said, "Come to me, all you who are weary and burdened, and I will give you rest" (Matt. 11:28). If the Son sets you free, you will be free indeed. To those who accept Him, He gives the right to become a child of God. Pray this prayer: "Lord Jesus, I am a sinner. I need redemption and for-giveness. I believe that You died on the cross for my sins. Will You forgive me and give me a clean heart and make me a child of God?"

I was so happy when I received my ticket a few days later. My finances are always in the realm of God's miracles. He is my heavenly Treasurer. When I need money—and I often do— I say to Him, "Father in heaven, in the Bible it says that You have cattle on a thousand hills. That's quite a lot. Will You sell Your cows and give me the money?" He always does so. I never need to ask people for money; I trust the Lord to tell them. This time, too, the money for the ticket arrived just on time. I leafed through my book of tickets with great thankfulness in my heart: "Formosa—Sydney—Auckland—Sydney—Tel Aviv—Cape Town—Amsterdam" . . . but that was different from what I had ordered!

I picked up the phone and said, "Miss, you've made a mistake. I ordered: Sydney, Cape Town and then Tel Aviv in Israel. And you've twisted that around. I don't make my travel plans myself; I ask God what His will is, and I want to obey Him."

"But the way you ordered your trip is impossible to arrange. There is no direct connection between Australia and South Africa. There are no islands in the Indian Ocean where a stopover can be made, so you first have to go to Tel Aviv and then Cape Town in South Africa." "So, that's the problem," I said, "Maybe we have to pray to God for an island in the Indian Ocean."

Half an hour later she phoned me. "Miss, did you pray for an island in the Indian Ocean? We just received a telegram from Quantas that they have leased Cocos Island, and you can now fly direct from Australia via Cocos Island to South Africa."

What wonderful music there is in following and obeying the Lord! God often specializes in the impossible. Hallelujah!

Let us pray: "Thank You, Lord, that we can tell You about our problems and ask You about everything. Thank You that You Yourself make us want to obey You. Lord, I thank You that You are listening to her and to him, who at this moment is saying, 'Lord Jesus, I want to be sure that I will go to heaven. I understand that You are calling me today to come to You. Lord, I come to You now and pray that You will forgive my sins, cleanse my heart, and prepare a place in the house with many mansions—the house of the Father. Thank You, Lord, that on the cross You accomplished everything to carry our—and also my—punishment; and that You have made me—yes, even me—a child of God. Hallelujah, what a Savior. Amen.'"

Afterword

The Corrie ten Boom House

Fulfilling Corrie ten Boom's dream of an "open house" like her family created, the Corrie ten Boom House and Museum in Haarlem, The Netherlands, was officially opened on April 15, 1988, exactly five years after Corrie's death. The house is less than an hour's trip by car or train from Amsterdam.

Amidst the bustling business district of Haarlem is the house that features the famous "hiding place," the basis of Corrie's well-known book and movie by the same name. The rooms are furnished as they were in the past, and there is also an exhibition about the Dutch resistance during World War II, along with a special display on Corrie's connection with the ministry of Trans World Radio. Just as when the Ten Boom family lived there, a clock and watch shop occupies the first floor—although it has since been modernized.

The house is operated by a foundation whose purpose is to keep the spiritual inheritance of the Ten Boom family alive as a sign and inspiration to present and future generations.

Tours through the house, located at 19 Barteljorisstraat, are given by volunteers (in English); operating hours are from 10 A.M. to 4 P.M. April 1–October 31, and from 11 A.M. to 3 P.M.

November 1–March 31. The house is closed on Sunday and Monday. Special appointments can be arranged for groups.

Admission to the house is free, although donations toward the continued preservation of the house are welcomed. All books written by or about Corrie ten Boom are available in the museum in various languages.

> *Corrie ten Boom House Haarlem Foundation*
> *P.O. Box 2237*
> *2002 CE Haarlem*
> *The Netherlands*
> *Tel: 31–23–5310823*

We want to hear from you. Please send your comments about this book to us in care of the address below. Thank you.

ZondervanPublishingHouse

Grand Rapids, Michigan
http://www.zondervan.com

A Division of HarperCollins*Publishers*